DREAMS

COMPANION STUDY GUIDE

13 LESSONS FOR INDIVIDUAL OR GROUP STUDY

SANDIE FREED

Melbourne, Florida USA

Dreams Companion Study Guide—Thirteen Lessons for Individual or Group Study

A Companion Study Guide to:
Sandie Freed. 2017. *Understanding Your Dreams*. Bloomington MN: Chosen Books.

Published by Parsons Publishing House
P. O. Box 410063
Melbourne, Florida 32941 USA
www.ParsonsPublishingHouse.com
Info@ParsonsPublishingHouse.com

Printed in the United States of America.

ISBN-13: 978-160273-061-8
ISBN-10: 1-60273-061-x
Printed in the United States of America.
For World-Wide Distribution.

INTRODUCTION

When I began to write about dreams and visions and how God has used them to change my life, I couldn't wait to throw myself completely into it! Dreams not only *saved* my life, but dreams and visions have been a constant to *transform* my life! Dreams and visions never stop speaking because God continues to speak, and He wants to use them to transform your life!

As you read my book, ***Understanding Your Dreams: How to Unlock the Meaning of God's Messages,*** you will find that using this practical and inspirational companion study guide will complete your journey to understanding what God is speaking to you! Yes, the Master Potter is shaping you and molding you…and He does this through your dreams and visions.

This study guide is written to enhance the revelation of your journey concerning God speaking through your dreams. Each chapter is guiding you toward not only understanding the purpose of this communication but how to hear His voice in the midst of them.

We designed this study guide so that you can take time to reflect, examine your heart, and be encouraged to move forward in faith. Also, it's an opportunity to expand your creativity—use crayons or colored pencils to create a beautiful palette that expresses God's design for your life. You can do this by coloring the designs created for you to express how you see the Savior working in your life.

Your study guide is also a workbook—study and then work it out on paper using whatever tool is needed. Work through your dreams and visions: journal your revelations, use colors to express your emotions, study the Bible verses, answer the questions, share your study points with others, ponder and meditate on the message. This is all about you…this is your expression!

As you pour over your text and meditate on your study guide, I expect nothing less than you developing more intimacy with God and realizing that He has been speaking to you in dreams and visions because He desires to heal you, transform you, deliver you, and relate to you!

My heart is to be your guide—your counselor and your spiritual director—through your dream world. Actually, it's His world…and He is inviting you in! Come with me and take a step with God.

Enjoy!

Dr. Sandie Freed

DREAMS ARE HEAVEN'S MESSAGES DOWNLOADED WHILE YOU SLEEP.

TABLE OF CONTENTS

GOD WARNS, DIRECTS, LEADS, AND GUIDES OUR STEPS THROUGH OUR DREAMS & VISIONS. THE WISDOM HE REVEALS THROUGH DREAMS WILL OPEN MANY DOORS OF OPPORTUNITY IN THE SEASON AHEAD.

HOW TO USE THIS STUDY GUIDE

Welcome to a life-changing study of **Understanding Your Dreams** (Chosen Books, 2017). This study guide is prepared to emphasize truths taught in our text, clarify your understanding, and prepare you to allow God to speak to you through visions and dreams. Thought-provoking questions and exercises inform and inspire in both individual and group settings.

LAYOUT TO LEARN

The layout of each chapter has eight sections to kindle your new knowledge specifically designed to supplement material contained in the text and take your understanding to new heights. Your study guide was designed with wide margins for note-taking and drawing with spaces for writing your answers so don't hesitate to customize it. Take time to ponder and meditate on the material and Bible verses as you color and personalize your study guide. Choose colors on pages 164-165 in your text to represent what God is speaking to you at the time. Get out your pens, pencils, and crayons along with your Bible and concordance to enjoy your transforming study.

Let me explain the purpose of each section.

DREAM TEXT

Highlights a significant passage from the text.

DREAM FOCUS

Explains the purpose of the chapter.

DREAM THINKING

Explores the topics with questions that emphasize important truths. Included are true/false, fill in the blank, short answer, lists, and open-ended questions.

DREAM APPLICATION

Assists you in applying the material you are studying.

DREAM ACTIVATION

Stimulates and motivates you as you walk in more knowledge.

DREAM SHARING

Discusses subjects that are appropriate in a group setting or just by yourself.

DREAM ANSWERS

Presents answers to questions along with possible answers for more insight. Study all the Bible verses included for more depth. If you don't remember the specific material, page numbers from the text will direct you to information you need.

DREAM JOURNALING

Outlet for recording and analyzing your dreams.

IN CONCLUSION

The best way to use this book is to USE this book to supplement the material in your text. If you don't use it, it won't help you. This study guide was developed with you in mind. Some questions may be more difficult to deal with especially if it involves deliverance; you might need to pray about your situation asking God to assist you in walking out your freedom and return to the question another day. If you come across a question you don't like, just press on; I believe the Holy Spirit will meet you where you are and take off the limits to where He wants to take you.

Activating the truths included in *Understanding Your Dreams* (Chosen Books, 2017) and this Study Guide are absolutely life-changing. With faith and patience, you can train yourself to wake up and record your dreams. With faith and patience, you can press into the message God is speaking to you when you dream. With faith and patience, you can help others discern their dreams. Understanding your dreams is an active pursuit. Dreams have in them the power to change your life; join me in this journey today.

LESSON 1

MEET THE MASTER POTTER

DREAM TEXT

If I told you that dreams and visions could utterly transform your life, would you take them more seriously? Would you pay more attention to them? What if I shared that a dream that someone else had about *me* literally saved my life? Or how about this: One night I overdosed on drugs. On the way to the hospital, I had a vision in which the Lord spoke to me very clearly and told me to choose life—and I did! In the vision I knew that if I did not choose life and change, I would die. Dear believer, I am alive today due to many diverse dreams and visions. And I want to share what I believe the Lord desires to do for *you* through them (*Understanding Your Dreams*, 19).

DREAM FOCUS

From our earliest biblical record, we see that God communicates with us through dreams. Scientists may not know why we dream, but we know that God uses dreams to speak to us. By reading the Word of God and sharing testimonies, we see that God continues to speak to us through dreams today.

There is a heavenly dream language that God uses to speak to us. He hides the meaning for us, not from us. It is up to us to be diligent to learn that language and how to interpret God's messages. Through this chapter, we see that God loves us, wants the best for us, and wants to communicate with us.

DREAM THINKING

1.   You may have many answers for this question, but focus on the text. What two things did I discuss that could completely transform your life TODAY?

   a._____

   b._____

I will
POUR
out
MY
SPIRIT
Joel 2:28

2. ☐ Yes ☐ No Are all dreams from God? Explain.

3. What do these names for God mean? Write one sentence of how He demonstrates this aspect of His character in your life.

El Shaddai – _____

_____

Emmanuel – _____

_____

Yahweh – _____

_____

Jehovah Rapha – _____

_____

4. When God speaks to us in a dream, do you automatically know what He is saying? Explain.

"

GOD LOVES
US SO MUCH THAT
HE IS NEVER NOT
PURSUING US.

"

5. When did God quit using dreams to speak to us?

6. Look at the dreams mentioned on page 22 in your text. What are your two favorite examples & why?

7. God is _____, and He speaks to us through _____ appointments.

8. Fill in the blank & determine what this statement means to you personally? "God _____ you, and His heart is to draw you continually _____ to Him."

9. You probably know many names for God. He is called the Master Potter & Master Weaver, what other names of God did I mention? Which name means the most to you today? Why?

_____ _____, _____,

_____, _____, and

_____.

REMEMBER:

*"God loves you &
His heart is to draw
you continually
nearer to Him."
~ Sandie Freed*

10.   In what Scripture passage do we read about God as the Master Potter? Think about this verse and tell how God is like the Master Potter.

11.   Explain what is wrong about this statement:

> *Dreams are an Old Testament phenomena that has passed away.*
> *God does not communicate through dreams any longer.*

DREAM APPLICATION

12.   I explained in my book how dreams have been part of my life story; how can dreams be part of your story?

13.   I've shared how God has been the Master Potter in my life. How has the Master Potter shown Himself in your life?

THE SPIRITUAL SOURCES OF TRUE DREAMS & VISIONS ARE ALWAYS MOTIVATED BY THE SPIRIT OF THE LORD AND COMMUNICATED THROUGH OUR NATURAL MINDS TO RELAY A DIVINE MESSAGE.

DREAM ACTIVATION

14.   In Daniel 1:17, we see where "God gave knowledge and understanding...And Daniel could understand visions and dreams of all kinds." How can you use this verse to help build your faith to understand your own dreams and visions?

15.   Discuss the importance of dreams and visions to God by examining how He used them from Jesus' birth up to preaching the gospel to the Gentiles. Look at the visions of Joseph (Mary's betrothed) and Peter, in particular. You can include other supernatural visitations if you like.

16.   Look up three Bible verses concerning how God has used dreams and meditate on it. Write the verses below.

DREAM SHARING

17. In chapter 1, I shared how some dreams and visions have changed the course of my life. Do you have some dreams and visions that have directed your life that you would like to share?

18. Sometimes we fail to understand or don't follow God's guidance through our dreams. Can you share any of the outcomes you have experienced in not following Him? In following Him?

DREAM ANSWERS - LESSON 1

1. Dreams & visions (p 19).
2. No, all dreams are not from God. Some can come from the natural man or soul. Dreams could also be false or demonically inspired dreams (Foreword, p. 11-13; p 53-55).
3. *El Shaddai* – "all sufficient One"; *Emmanuel* – "God with us"; *Yahweh* – "I Am"; *Jehovah Rapha* – "the God that heals" (p 24). Varies.
4. No, you do not. You need tools such as your text and this book to help us understand God's dream language. Also, we must actively pursue God's message through prayer and discernment. You may also consult a person you respect and know to give you Biblical guidance. God's mysteries are hidden for you—not from you. (p 20-21).
5. He didn't; God still speaks to us through dreams today (p 21).
6. Varies (p 22).
7. Supernatural ; supernatural/divine (p 23).
8. Loves & nearer (p 23). Varies.
9. The Rock, the Vine, the Good Shepherd, the Lamb & the Door (p 24). Varies.
10. Jer 18:1-6 (p 24, 26). God is like a Master Potter in that He will take the imperfections in your life & through His divine guidance, He will mold you into His image IF you allow it (p 25).
11. It is said in Jude that dreams and visions from God would play an important role in the last days. God used dreams to communicate with Joseph about the birth of his son, Jesus. It could be said that the dreams given to Joseph were still under the Old Testament covenant; however, the visions given to Peter about sharing the gospel with the gentiles were most certainly New Testament and apply to us today. God uses dreams and visions in other New Testament passages (p 19).
12. Dreams are used to direct, guide, correct & give you comfort. God wants to speak to you clearly through dreams which will lead you to fulfill your divine destiny (p 20).
13. Varies.
14. You can build your faith that the Lord will help you understand His message because He did it for Daniel. If He did it for Daniel, He'll do it for you (p 22-23).
15. God spoke to Joseph about God's Son being born to Mary and the steps he needed to take to protect the newborn Savior. These events were critical in the coming of our Lord to establish His safety and to fulfill prophecy. Another critical time the Lord needed to speak past social and religious ideology was when it was time to include the Gentiles in the church; God used a vision that got Peter's attention and gave Him confidence to pursue this controversial action (p 20).
16. You can choose verses from page 22 of your text or look up verses yourself. Varies.
17. Varies.
18. Varies.

DREAM JOURNALING

Ask God to speak to you through dreams. Take time this week to record your dreams as soon as you wake up—even if it's in the middle of the night. Include as many details as you can to describe what you dream. Keep pen and paper or an electronic device at your bedside to record what you remember. Ask the Lord to help you do this. It takes time to form a dream journaling habit. Don't try to interpret it now; we'll discuss this later.

Day 1:

Day 2:

I LIKE TO TELL PEOPLE
THAT GOD HAS TO SPEAK TO ME
DURING DREAMS SO THAT
I WON'T TALK BACK.

LESSON 2

GOD IS A TALKING GOD

DREAM TEXT

Think about this: From the time of our creation, God purposefully placed within each one of His children the divine ability to hear His voice! He expects us to hear Him, and this proves He wants to talk to us. When I think about this, I visualize a Holy Ghost radio tower that is transmitting heaven's language, and placed within me is a receiver, like an antenna, that directly tunes me in to hear His voice. This supernatural device gives me a direct line to my Father, and when He talks, I want to listen (*Understanding Your Dreams*, 51-52).

DREAM FOCUS

In this chapter, I want to emphasize to you that God still speaks today. He spoke in the past; He speaks today; He will speak tomorrow. It is His desire to communicate to His people, and one way He does this is through supernatural dreams. As we desire this interaction, it is essential to prepare our hearts to receive from God. Dreams come to us like parables—illustrated stories—while we sleep. The message is not always clear, but through faith, patience, and discernment, God will speak to us. Don't limit how He speaks. Open your heart and mind to receive from Him through dreams and visions!

DREAM THINKING

1. On page 40 of your text, I reveal the secret tools that God used over the years to bring about my emotional healing and deliverance. What were these? How has God used these two tools in your life?

   1)_____

   2)_____

REMEMBER:

"We must exercise spiritual discernment when receiving and interpreting dreams and visions."
~ Sandie Freed

2.   ☐ True   ☐ False   God only speaks to super spiritual people.
      Answer this question and then list a Scripture verse(s) that supports or refutes
      it.

3.   In this chapter, I discuss the difference between dreams and visions. The purpose
      of dreams is to connect with God's _____. God uses visions
      to reveal His _____.

4.   In 1 Kings 3:5-14, we see that Solomon received an _____
      of wisdom in his dream.

5.   Dreams are full of symbols when you are _____, and visions
      usually include a more clear message when you are _____.

6.   What is a supernatural encounter with God, and why is it important?

7.   Concerning dreams and visions, I like to say, "Nothing is always." Explore what I mean by this statement?

8.   Science tells us that dreams come during the REM (rapid eye movement) cycle of our sleep, and on average, adults may dream three to five times per night. What is the best method for you to determine if the messages of these dreams are connected to each other? _____. Explain your answer.

9.   ☐ True ☐ False   Defining an event as a dream, vision, etc. is not as important as the fact that God is speaking to you.

10.   Is this statement true: God only speaks through dreams and visions? Explain.

11.   It is great to testify about how God has spoken to you through dreams. The word "testimony" means: _____.
Explain how your testimony can help others.

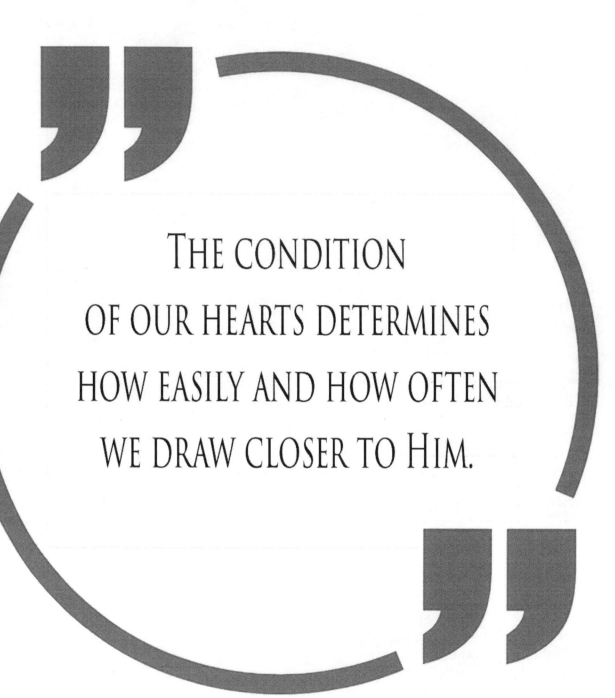

THE CONDITION
OF OUR HEARTS DETERMINES
HOW EASILY AND HOW OFTEN
WE DRAW CLOSER TO HIM.

12. God will speak to us in many different ways if we will be people with open

     _____ and open _____.

13. If we are close-minded, God will be unable to communicate with us through certain methods. How does this work?

14. How can your hearing become dull to God's voice?

DREAM APPLICATION

15. If you listen to daytime TV, they say (like I used to do) people are nuts if you think God speaks to you. How would you respond to that statement? Take time to pray for the courage to stand up for the truth at the proper time.

16. We've talked a lot about how God uses dreams to speak to us. Again, I ask is every dream from God? What is a major key to avoid making an error with a dream?

DREAM ACTIVATION

17.   This is an exercise to build your faith that God wants to communicate with you. Ponder and meditate on John 10:27. Repeat this verse emphasizing one word at a time. Say: "MY sheep hear My voice, and I know them, and they follow Me." "My SHEEP hear My voice, and I know them, and they follow Me." "My sheep HEAR My voice, and I know them, and they follow Me." Continue on with the rest of the verse. Write your personal revelations. Do any other Bible verses come to mind?

18.   Your future in God is bright! Prepare your heart to receive God's message to you by taking time to meditate on Jeremiah 29:11, which says "'For I know the plans I have for you,' says the LORD. 'They are plans for good and not for disaster, to give you a future and a hope.'" Answer these questions as you meditate. Write down any thoughts or revelations you have.

    a)   Who is speaking? _____

    b)   What does He know (He's not thinking or wishing; He knows)? _____

    c)   Are the plans for our good or bad? _____

    d)   Why does He have plans? _____

GOD IS REVEALING HIS PERFECT WILL FOR US THROUGH DREAMS. HE IS LIFTING THE VEIL OFF OF WHAT HAS BEEN HIDDEN AND REVEALING PRAYER STRATEGY FOR OUR SEASON AHEAD.

DREAM SHARING

19.   On page 39 in the text, I shared about how God saved me from my suicide attempt when I was 16 years old. Following that, I heard in Sunday school that God loved me and was full of grace toward me. I wrote, "Knowing I could hear His voice, that He loved me, that He obviously had a destiny for me to fulfill empowered me that day to move forward in life and seek Him more." Share your experience when you realized God had a destiny for you and you wanted to pursue it. If you have never experienced that, re-reread pages 39-40 to find out about God's wondrous love for you.

20.   Share some dreams or visions that you have experienced and what God was saying or revealing to you.

DREAM ANSWERS - LESSON 2

1. 1) dreams; 2) visions (p 40).
2. False (p 40-41). "I am the good shepherd; and I know My sheep, and am known by My own" (Jn 10:14). "My sheep hear my voice" (Jn 10:27). Varies.
3. Heart; nature (p 42).
4. Impartation (p 43).
5. Asleep; awake, (p 45).
6. A supernatural encounter is basically God communicating to us. It could be through a dream, vision, prophecy, angelic visitation, God's audible voice, prayer, etc. It is important for you to get your guidance from heaven and for God to communicate with you in order to mold and shape you into His image (p 44).
7. "Nothing is always" means that there are no definitives in dream interpretation. There is no symbol that ALWAYS means the same thing no matter who dreamed it or where. This statement helps keep you open to God's unique message—even when He uses a familiar symbol; God's goal is to press you to seek Him for His divine message at that moment in time (p 45).
8. Journal. Journaling helps you order your understanding about the dreams God gives you. By journaling, you are better able to follow the connections of your dreams (p 46).
9. True. It doesn't matter what you call it; the important thing is the message. However, studying the various ways God speaks will build your faith to hear Him when He does (p 49).
10. No. God speaks in many ways: inner "witness", rhema, logos, etc. (p 50).
11. "Do it again, God!" Testimonies can be used to build the faith of the hearers which will allow God to do it again in their lives as He has done for others (p 51). Varies.
12. Minds; hearts (p 51).
13. If we don't have the faith for God to speak to us using dreams and visions, we won't be aware of His message when it comes. If we say God no longer grants visions to people, there is no way that we would hear Him because we've ruled out that avenue for Him to use (p 51-52).
14. Unrepented sin can muffle your hearing (p 52).
15. Various. God does still speak today because the Bible says that His sheep hear His voice (Jn 10:27). We see Him continuing to speak to people in the New Testament, and there was never a moment when He said that He was no longer going to communicate with people. The Book of Acts is still being written in heaven (p 51-52).
16. No. Some dreams are soulish dreams or demon-inspired. Submit your heart and mind to the Lord and wait patiently for the God-given interpretation (p 53-54).
17. Varies.
18. a) God; b) He knows the plans He has for you; c) His plans are for your good; d) He has plans that give you a future and a hope. That's great news!
19. Varies.
20. Varies.

DREAM JOURNALING

Take time to record your dreams again this week. Continue to include as many details as you can to describe what you dreamed. Keep something near you to record your dream without waking up too much. Ask the Lord to help you. Keep working to establish your dream journaling habit. We'll consider the interpretation of the dream later. Color and decorate your study guide as you are inspired.

Dream 1:

Dream 2:

> A DREAM IS ANOTHER
> GOD ENCOUNTER—SO LISTEN!
> DON'T TREAT YOUR DREAMS
> LIKE JUNK MAIL ANYMORE.
> DREAMS ARE IMPORTANT.

LESSON 3

GOD CHANGES OUR HEARTS THROUGH DREAMS AND VISIONS

DREAM TEXT

I believe that God's entire purpose for using dreams and visions is to continue to align our hearts, thoughts, lives, and intentions with His eternal plan. I have heard it said, and it is very true, that dreams and visions are God's love language (*Understanding Your Dreams*, 60).

DREAM FOCUS

As you build your foundation for understanding dreams, I chose this chapter to demonstrate how God will use dreams and visions to reveal your true self—your spiritual heart. I shared my personal experience about how I was literally killing myself, and God spoke to me through a dream that changed my life. Through dreams, God purposes to lead and guide you into His perfect will for your life. Nebuchadnezzar's experience with the Lord is a great example to study.

DREAM THINKING

1. "God's entire purpose for using dreams and visions is_____
_____
_____."

2. In question 1 above, you recited my thoughts about God's divine purpose for using dreams and visions in our lives. What are your own thoughts about why He might use dreams and visions?

For God does speak—

now one way, now another—

though no one perceives it.

In a dream, in a vision of the night,

when deep sleep falls on people

as they slumber in their beds,

he may speak in their ears

and terrify them with warnings,

to turn them from wrongdoing

and keep them from pride,

to preserve them from the pit,

their lives from perishing by the sword.

(Job 33:14-18)

3.   According to Job 33:14-18, why does God want to speak to us?

a. _____

b. _____

c. _____

4.   It can be difficult for you to see these two dangerous sins in your own life: _____ and _____.

5.   For what purpose did Daniel say God gave him the interpretation for King Nebuchadnezzar's dream? Is it easy to know what's in your own heart?

6.   If you have yet to study Daniel chapters 2-5 in your Bible, take time to do that now. In these chapters, we see how God tried to speak to Kings Nebuchadnezzar and Belshazzar about their spiritual hearts. Read the passages and look for the moments when God is reaching out to these kings through supernatural means. List the times God tried to speak to them in these chapters. What is an overarching theme here?

a) _____

b) _____

c) _____

d) _____

e) _____

Theme: _____

_____

7.   According to Daniel 2:27-28, the Bible says, "Daniel replied, 'No wise man, enchanter, magician or diviner can explain to the king the mystery he has asked about, but there is a God in heaven who reveals mysteries.'" Who reveals mysteries to you when you sleep?

_____

> "I HAVE LEARNED
> TO BE PATIENT WHENEVER
> I AM INTERPRETING DREAMS.
> SYMBOLISM OFTEN REQUIRES
> TIME TO INTERPRET."

40   Lesson 3

8.   Repentance is turning _____ sin and _____ God.

9.   God's grace helped King Nebuchadnezzar realize his haughty pride and idolatry. What was Nebuchadnezzar's response?

10.   Until we reach heaven, repentance and deliverance are always a work in progress for us. How did God reward Nebuchadnezzar for acknowledging that He rules and reigns?

11.   Define idolatry: _____

    _____

12.   In the first Commandment, God said to have no other gods before Him. In other words, we are to avoid idolatry. Use page 63 of my book to rewrite this commandment in your own words.

13.   How can you avoid creating or worshipping a false image of the Lord (idol)?

WHEN WE HEAR FROM GOD, WE MUST ALSO ACT UPON WHAT WE HEAR; OTHERWISE WE WILL CONTINUE TO REMAIN IN OUR PAST AND NEVER MOVE FORWARD INTO A PLACE OF ENLARGEMENT & INCREASE.

14.   Is it considered a form of idolatry when we view ourselves differently than God views us? Why?

15.   In my book *Silencing the Accuser: Eight Lies Satan Uses Against Christians*, I talk about combatting the false identity that Satan wants us to have about ourselves. How can you accomplish this?

a)_____

b)_____

DREAM APPLICATION

16.   God loves us and wants to change us from the inside out for our good and His glory. Only He knows what's in our true spiritual heart. Take the time here to consider any short-comings that God possibly has been dealing with you about through a dream or other method. Write about three areas where He is dealing with you and Scripture verses to help you overcome them.

a)_____

b)_____

c)_____

17.   What does the Bible say about you as a believer? Make a list of some things the Word says about you and look up Bible verses upon which you may meditate and ponder.

FOR GOD SO LOVED the WORLD
John 3:16

DREAM ACTIVATION

18. A God-given dream or vision is often one of God's initial steps in revealing areas that need to change. After that revelation, you must rely on God's grace to grow through the challenge into freedom. Utilize this list on how to move from bondage to freedom:

    I. Always and foremost: understand God loves you (meditate on Scriptures that reveal God's love for YOU!). REMEMBER: He who knows you best, loves you most!!

        a. "For God so loved [insert your name] that He gave His only begotten Son" (Jn 3:16).

        b. "If God is for [insert your name], who can be against [insert your name]?" (Ro 8:31).

    II. Become aware of the problem (this may come as a result of self-evaluation or God's intervention through dreams, visions, etc.)

    III. Acknowledge your need for change. If you're not ready to change, ask God to help you get ready. Just like the father said to Jesus, "Lord, I believe; help my unbelief! (Mark 9:24). If you're struggling with the desire to change, pray: "Lord, I know I need to change; please help me want to change."

    IV. Seek God's supernatural help and divine grace: PRAY.

    V. Renew your mind to the Word of God (find verses to help your weaknesses)

    VI. Keep thanking God and worshipping Him until your freedom comes. NEVER EVER give up!!

19. Only God knows what is in your heart, and He loves you enough to want to see you change. In question 16, I asked you to consider any shortcomings that God has shown you. List Bible verses for your forgiveness.

REMEMBER:
"God is a talking God!"
~ Sandie Freed

DREAM SHARING

20.   I shared an account where God gave me an open vision that resulted in my healing from an out-of-control eating disorder. God brought me down a path to freedom, but it all started with a vision. If you think back to your own life, has God ever given you a life-changing vision or dream? Did you take actions or are you taking actions to make that change? Contemplate what you can do to continue walking in freedom.

DREAM ANSWERS - LESSON 3

1. "To continue to align our hearts, thoughts, lives and intentions with His eternal plan" (p 60).
2. Varies.
3. a) Turn us from wrongdoing; b) keep us from pride; c) preserve our souls (p 61).
4. Haughtiness; pride (p 61).
5. In Daniel 2:30 (KJV), Daniel said "that thou [King Nebuchadnezzar] mightest know the thoughts of thy heart" (p 61). No, it's not easy to know what's in our own hearts. The Bible says, "The heart is deceitful above all things and beyond cure. Who can understand it?" (Jer 17:9). Only God knows your heart (Lk 16:15; Jn 2:25; Acts 15:8).
6. a) Dream (Dan 2:1); b) vision (Dan 4:13); c) voice (Dan 4:31); d) handwriting (Dan 5:5).
   Theme: God will humble whom He humbles (Dan 4:37; Dan 5:19) (p 61-62).
7. God reveals the mysteries to the interpretation of dreams (p 61-62).
8. From; to (p 62).
9. He honored God. The king saw the depth of his pride when he hit rock bottom and humbled himself. Thank God for His grace and how He's willing to speak to us to prompt a change (p 62).
10. Once the King acknowledged God's sovereignty, his kingdom was restored. It was promised in Dan 4:26, and God did it in Dan 4:36 (p 62).
11. Idolatry: Pride in our own abilities (p 63).
12. Varies. Have no false images before you. Have a biblical view of God and yourself (p 63).
13. Allow your image of God to be defined by the Bible—not man's traditions (p 63). As you worship the one true God, you will not fall for an imitation!
14. Yes. If we view ourselves as anything other than what God says about us, it is a "false image" of yourself and thereby "idolatry" by definition (p 64).
15. a) Believe what the Bible says about you; b) repent from idolatry (p 63-64).
16. Varies.
17. Varies. New creation (2 Cor 5:17), His workmanship (Eph 2:10), royal priesthood (1 Pe 2:9), children of God (Jn 1:12), body is the temple of the Holy Spirit (1 Cor 6:19), friends of God (Jn 15:15), seated in heavenly places with Christ Jesus (Eph 2:6), sons of God (Ga 4:6), transformed (Ro 12:2), heir of God (Ro 8:17), blessed (Eph 1:3), forgiven (Eph 1:7), ambassador for Christ (2 Cor 5:20), eternal life (Ro 6:23), etc.
18. Varies.
19. "If we confess our sins, he is faithful and just and will forgive us our sins and purify us from all unrighteousness" (1 Jn 1:9). "And forgive us our debts, as we also have forgiven our debtors" (Matt 6:12). "All the prophets testify about him that everyone who believes in him receives forgiveness of sins through his name" (Acts 10:43). "In him we have redemption through his blood, the forgiveness of sins, in accordance with the riches of God's grace" (Eph 1:7; Col 1:14).
20. Varies.

DREAM JOURNALING

Continue to develop your dream journaling habit by taking time to record your dreams again this week. Pay attention to details and include as many as you can to describe what you dreamed. Ask the Lord to help you. We'll study interpretation later. Continue to use various colors throughout this guide to help you ponder what God is showing you.

Dream 1:

Dream 2:

Do not be conformed to this world (this age), [fashioned after and adapted to its external, superficial customs], but be transformed (changed) by the [entire] renewal of your mind [by its new ideals and its new attitude], so that you may prove [for yourselves] what is the good and acceptable and perfect will of God, even the thing which is good and acceptable and perfect [in His sight for you]

(Romans 12:2, AMPC).

LESSON 4

DREAMS REVEAL HIDDEN MYSTERIES

DREAM TEXT

For us to fully receive God's truths, especially through dreams and visions, our minds must become fashioned by Him and renewed. With that in mind, know that as you continue to read, the Master Potter is at work, molding and fashioning you and your mind. You are being transformed. There is much to learn concerning your destiny and how God desires to bless you! (*Understanding Your Dreams*, 66).

DREAM FOCUS

This is one of the most important chapters where we discuss God's desire to reveal hidden secrets to us—to YOU! As we are fashioned into His image with His heart, His desires, His thoughts, God is more able to share the mysteries of the Universe with us. Our responsibility in the divine molding and shaping process is an active pursuit of God Himself through worship and His Word. It's important for you to take time to understand who you are in Christ so you can discern His presence. As you study God's relationship with Jeremiah, your faith will soar to experience heavenly visions and dreams.

DREAM THINKING

1.   Up to this point, I've discussed two reasons God gives us dreams and visions. What are they?

2.   This lesson contains my comparison of the purpose of revelation to that of a compass. How can revelation be like a compass?

3.   In this chapter, I discuss one reason why God may hide things from us. Discuss this reason.

4.   Think about and discuss how God uses symbols and mysteries to show us His love. Include a Bible verse to support your answer.

5.   Can you interpret God's dream language without prayer? Explain.

WE SHOULD NEVER TREAT OUR DREAMS AS UNIMPORTANT, BUT RATHER FINETUNE OUR SPIRITUAL SENSES TO HEAR HIS VOICE MORE ACCURATELY.

6.   In the dreams that God gives, does He usually speak directly or through symbolism?

7.   How can you determine the symbolism behind your dreams and visions?

8.   God's mysteries require our pursuit. Think of three ways that will help you pursue revelation about the mysteries God shows you.

REMEMBER:

"As I have written repeatedly, dream language is about a loving God who continually, obstinately and passionately pursues His people."
~ Sandie Freed

9. God has shown His character in the Bible—how He thinks, how He works, and how He deals with His children. Like most of us, we tend to react true to our character. Is it God's nature to speak to His sons and daughters while refusing to give them understanding? Discuss this and include Bible verses to justify your answer.

10. How are your dreams and visions like treasure hunts? Have you had the Lord continue to remind you of a dream and drive you to understand it?

11. Romans 8:17 says you are a joint-heir with Jesus Christ. In your own words, write about the inheritance you receive when becoming a Christian. Include various Scripture verses.

OPEN the EYES of my HEART! EPHESIANS 1:18

12. I am so adamant about learning who you are in Christ because of my past identity issues that bound me for years. Why are there many Christians having an identity crisis?

13. Salvation means having everything heaven has to offer. Explain how salvation brings you deliverance. List Scripture examples.

14. Dreams are like the _____ of Jesus with the meaning of them _____.

15. Jesus desires to _____ what He has _____.

16. Revelation 5:9-10 says that He has made us kings and priests. Is it possible to earn or be worthy of this position on your own?

> In our dreams, God will give specific direction about which doors to walk through. Yes, the enemy can open doors also, but a dream will reveal if it is the one that will benefit or hinder us.

17.   God hides mysteries for us, not from us. If you read Proverbs 25:2 along with Mark 4:22-25, you will see God's purpose is not to confuse or keep you in the dark about His mysteries. Using these verses, explain how it is God's will to reveal and your privilege to press into Him for the revelation.

18.   How can you train yourself to have ears to hear as mentioned in Mark 4:9, 23; Mark 8:18; Luke 8:8; Romans 11:8; Revelation 2:11, Deuteronomy 29:4?

19.   As I said in your text, ***Understanding Your Dreams***, take the time to read Jeremiah 1:5-12. Answer these questions below. My revelation of this passage can be found on pages 72-74 of the text.

    a) How did Jeremiah see himself?

    b) Describe how God saw Jeremiah.

    c) What did God do to Jeremiah's mouth?

    d) What did Jeremiah see after this?

    e) What did God promise to do?

REMEMBER:

"*Your dream can originate from several sources and, in fact, may not be from God.*"
~ Sandie Freed

20.   Read and meditate on the acronym for worship that I included in your text on page 75. Write what God is speaking to you about each letter.

W

_____

O

_____

R

_____

S

_____

H

_____

I

_____

P

DREAM APPLICATION

21.   Read and meditate on Ephesians chapter 1. Answer these questions to help you apply this truth to your life.

1) How has God blessed you?

2) When did He choose you?

3) For what purpose did He choose you?

4) What has He made known to you?

5) Why did He do all these things?

6) With what seal have you been marked?

EXERCISE YOUR SENSES to discern GOOD & EVIL

He 5:14

7) In Ephesians 1:17-19, Paul prayed that God would grant you revelation. List 4 of the reasons why he prayed this:

8) What power did Jesus give you by His Spirit?

9) Who is the head of the church?

22.   Read through the parable in Mark 4:1-9. Practice interpreting this parable by jumping ahead to the symbolism dictionary in chapter 9 (p. 155 of the text). Does your interpretation make sense? You can read further in Mark 4:13-20 to confirm your answer.

Farmer _____

Seed _____

Path _____

Bird _____

DREAM ACTIVATION

23.   On pages 74-75 of our text, I share with you how to activate visions through worship. Take time to re-read these pages and enter into worship and hear what God speaks to you.

REMEMBER:

"*Nothing is always when interpreting dreams. By that I mean that no particular symbol means the same thing.*"
~ *Sandie Freed*

DREAM SHARING

24. I wrote about dreams that brought me deliverance from shame, inadequacy, and lack of fulfillment. Thank God for dreams!! Think about any dreams you have had recently and prayerfully determine if God is revealing strongholds in your own life.

25. Take time to think about and share the most life-changing truth you experienced when you received salvation. Can you find a Scripture verse that promises this experience to everyone?

DREAM ANSWERS - LESSON 4

1. 1) To reveal what is in our heart; 2) to reveal hidden mysteries to us (p 66).
2. It challenges us to change our course and head toward our true north (p 66).
3. So we will draw near Him to seek the answers (p 66).
4. God uses His dream language to draw you closer to Him. Understanding His mysteries is totally dependent upon His love for you and the relationship you have with Him. He hides His secrets for you, not from you. Your relationship with God is the key element when interpreting dreams (p 67-68). See John 15-16.
5. No. You must have prayer because God's ways are not always your ways, and His thoughts are not always your thoughts. You must have God's involvement to determine what He is saying. God must shed His light on our dreams to bring understanding (p 67).
6. Symbolism; Jesus always used parables and stories to explain things to help the disciples understand Kingdom mysteries (see Mt 13:11-15; Mk 4:10-14) (p 69-70).
7. Pray to hear His voice, and pursue revelation from God (p 67).
8. 1) Seek God through prayer and worship; 2) reading the Word; 3) educate yourself as to how God has spoken in the past (p 74).
9. No. It's not God's nature to show you something and then not tell you what it means. "Ask and it will be given to you; seek and you will find; knock and the door will be opened to you" (Mt 7:7). If we ask, He will tell us—in His timing, but He will do it. "For whatever is hidden is meant to be disclosed, and whatever is concealed is meant to be brought out into the open" (Mk 4:22). "You have heard these things; look at them all. Will you not admit them? 'From now on I will tell you of new things, of hidden things unknown to you'" (Is 48:6). "He reveals deep and hidden things; he knows what lies in darkness, and light dwells with him" (Dan 2:22). "I praise you, Father, Lord of heaven and earth, because you have hidden these things from the wise and learned, and revealed them to little children" (Mt 11:25). Varies (p 70-71).
10. Dreams are mysteries with clues to bring us to a heavenly prize or message. Varies (p 67).
11. As a child of God, your inheritance gives you or makes you: EVERY spiritual blessing (Eph 1:3); eternal life (1 Jn 2:25, Mt 19:29); freedom from sin and death (Ro 8:2); saints of God (1 Cor 1:2, KJV); alive in Christ (1 Cor 15:22); anointing (2 Cor 1:21); triumphant (2 Cor 2:14, KJV); new creation (2 Cor 5:17); child of God (Ga 3:26); seated together in heavenly places with Christ (Eph 2:6); brought near (Eph 2:13); health (3 Jn 1:2). Varies (p 68-70).
12. Because they don't know who they are in Christ. They are already righteous due to the completed work of Jesus. You cannot prove your value; Jesus has already done that due to the fact that He died for you (p 68).
13. Through Jesus, we receive salvation (*sozo*) which means saved, healed, delivered, prosperous, protected, supported, and set free. Examples: woman with issue of blood (Mk 5:29), healed leper (Mk 1:42), healed girl (Mk 5:34), set captives free (Lk 4:18), set free demon possessed man (Mt 8:28-34), etc. Varies (p 68).
14. Parables; hidden/mysterious (p 69-70).
15. Reveal; concealed (p 70).
16. No. Jesus has made you worthy, and it is He that has made you a king and a priest by grace through faith (p 70-71).
17. Proverbs 25:2 says the Lord may hide something for you, but it's up to you to search out the meaning as a king and a priest unto God. Christians should always press into Him and that closeness will reveal hidden mysteries. Don't just throw your hands up and say you don't understand; seek Him, and He will reveal it to you (p 71-72).
18. Open yourself to God's revelation to hear God's heavenly message with a spiritual ear (p 70-71).
19. a) Jeremiah thought he was too young and didn't know how to speak. b) The Lord reprimanded Jeremiah and told him that he had been set apart to be over the nations as a prophet. c) The Lord touched Jeremiah's mouth and gave him the ability to speak on His behalf. d) Jeremiah saw an almond tree branch. e) God promised to fulfill His Word in Jeremiah's life (p 72-74).
20. Varies (p 75).
21. From Ephesians 1: 1) With every spiritual blessing in Christ (v 3); 2) Before the foundation of the world (v 4); 3) To be holy & blameless (v 4); 4) the mysteries of His will (v 10); 5) to bring unity (v 10); 6) The Spirit (v 13); 7) To know Him better, the hope of my calling, the riches of His inheritance, His great power (v 17-19); 8) His mighty strength (v 19); 9) Christ (v 22). Varies (p 68-69).
22. Farmer: You/spiritual leader; Seed: the Word; Path/Soil: Heart; Bird: Satan/evil (p 70-71).
23. Varies.   24. Varies.   25. Varies.

DREAM JOURNALING

Continue to develop your dream journaling habit by using this dream journal page. Feel free to make copies of it. Include as many details as you can to describe what you dreamed. Ask the Lord to help you. We'll study interpretation in chapters 7 and 8. Continue to sketch and color your thoughts and revelations throughout this book.

Dream 1:

Dream 2:

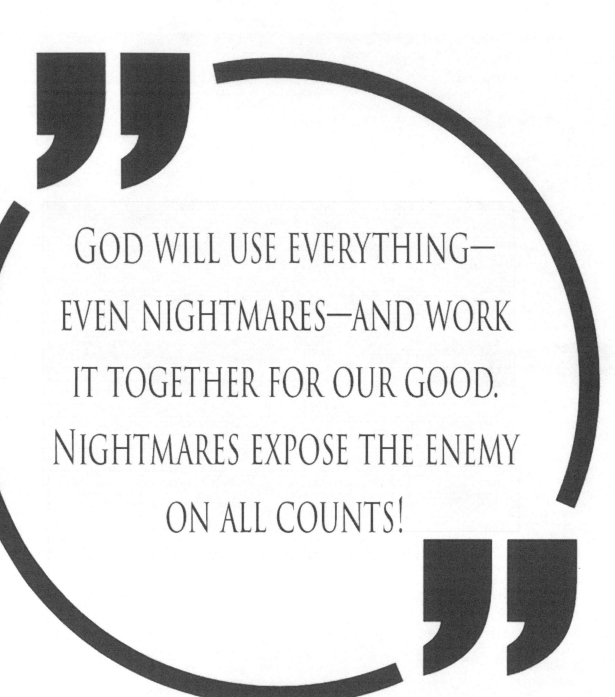

GOD WILL USE EVERYTHING—
EVEN NIGHTMARES—AND WORK
IT TOGETHER FOR OUR GOOD.
NIGHTMARES EXPOSE THE ENEMY
ON ALL COUNTS!

LESSON 5

DREAMS THAT INFLUENCE OUR DESTINY

DREAM TEXT

Dreams from the Holy Spirit reveal God's ultimate plan for our lives (even though interpretations may take a while!). They counsel us along the way, they speak truth into hidden places that have concealed lies, and they lead us along paths of righteousness. In 1 Corinthians 14:3 we read that the spirit of prophecy is meant for edification, exhortation and comfort. This, then, will be our plumb line for interpreting dreams from the Holy Spirit (*Understanding Your Dreams*, 80).

DREAM FOCUS

This chapter introduces categories of dreams that God uses to impact destiny. In this chapter, I share many of my personal dreams and the interpretation as it came to me. Pay close attention to the types of dreams while understanding two foundational principles: nothing is always and remember who the Holy Spirit is according to Scripture.

DREAM THINKING

1.   Read and meditate on Jeremiah 29:11. Answer these questions to help you apply this truth to your life.
    a) Is it a certainty that God has plans for your life?

    b) The plans the Lord has for you include 4 things. List below:

REMEMBER:

"*When documenting and interpreting dreams the Holy Spirit is your guide.*"
~ *Sandie Freed*

2.   In this chapter, we looked at the word "destiny" and its definition. The King James translation defines God's promise of destiny as an _____ _____.

3.   What is a destiny dream?

4.   With dreams, God reveals hidden _____, but He also wants to _____ us today with a plan to move us forward to fulfill His destiny for us.

5.   How is having a destiny dream like when Israel entered the Promised Land?

6.   Holy Spirit dreams will always grant you _____ and _____.

7.   What is a basic principle when interpreting dreams?

8.   Dreams and visions from God will give you supernatural _____ to know things and release an _____to understand.

> # "The devil loves to intimidate God's children because it keeps us from stepping out with boldness & confidence as we teach or demonstrate the Word."

9.   Dreams, like the spirit of prophecy, are given for edification, exhortation, and comfort. Define these words below. You may want to gain a greater depth of each word by consulting a dictionary.

_____

Edify

_____

Exhort

_____

Comfort

10.   In this chapter, I teach about dreams with recurring themes on pages 83-93 in your text. Why does God give us this type of dream?

11.   You might dream about a school if God wants you to _____ something.

12.   When interpreting a dream it's important to examine the details. What details might be important to observe if you were dreaming about being in school?

13.   Dreams about vehicles are very important. These dreams could possibly represent:

_____.

14. What is the basic principle that I discuss throughout your text that you should remember in your relationship with God—especially as it relates to dream interpretation?

15. God dreams never bring _____.

16. Most dreams are intrinsic in nature, meaning they concern your core-being—your inner (inward) man. Most of the time, God is dealing with your _____, _____, _____, _____, etc.

17. Why is it never appropriate to have a legalistic approach to interpreting dreams?

18. It's so easy to jump to conclusions when interpreting dreams—especially for the novice. Remember: NOTHING IS ALWAYS. The common dream interpretations that I share in your text are just that—common, but not always the case. Why should you always take time to seek God with dream interpretations for yourself or others?

"For I know the plans I have for you," declares the Lord, "plans to prosper you and not to harm you, plans to give you hope and a future. Then you will call on me and come and pray to me, and I will listen to you. You will seek me and find me when you seek me with all your heart. I will be found by you," declares the Lord, "and will bring you back from captivity.
(Jeremiah 29:11-14).

19. On page 99 in your text, I talk about the prophetic influence of directive dreams. Why does God give directive dreams?

DREAM APPLICATION

20. Re-read and meditate on Jeremiah 29:11. As you read it, emphasize one word at a time, and then repeat emphasizing the next word. What is God saying to you as you read this? Does this verse stir up HOPE in your spirit?

21. The types of dreams I share in this chapter are really the foundation for dream interpretation. Study these types and become thoroughly familiar with the different categories. List five categories and what they could mean.

    1)

    _____

    2)

    _____

    3)

    _____

    4)

    _____

    5)

    _____

REMEMBER:

"Your dreams and visions bring not only revelation but also an impartation."
~ Sandie Freed

22. As I mention on page 89 in your text, self-talk is critically important in the life of a believer. Think about whether your self-talk is positive and biblical or negative and full of doubt. Write down three instances of how your own self-talk could be improved. If you don't practice self-talk, you need to start that habit now.

    1)

    _____

    2)

    _____

    3)

DREAM ACTIVATION

23. Mediate on the names for the Spirit below and find the Bible verses where He is identified as such. Add other names to this list. Which of these mean the most to you at this moment in time?

    1) Breath: _____

    2) Comforter: _____

    3) Counselor: _____

    4) Advocate: _____

    5) Convicts us of sin: _____

    6) Intercessor; _____

    7) Revealer: _____

    8) Spirit of Truth: _____

    9) Teacher: _____

    "I need the Holy Spirit as _____ to me now because _____."

DANIEL had UNDERSTANDING in all VISIONS & DREAMS

Dan1:17

24. In life, you will often have to encourage yourself as you pursue God's purposes, like King David did in 1 Samuel 30:6. Take time to look at this verse in several translations to get the full depth of it. Write out five encouraging scripts/confessions that you would benefit from hearing yourself repeat. Start a daily habit of quoting these biblical encouragements. As different things come up, you will find that you can add new statements and possibly quit using others.

    1)

    _____

    2)

    _____

    3)

    _____

    4)

    _____

    5)

    _____

25. As I mention on page 89 in your text, some dreams are from God and some are demonically inspired. When you wake up from a dream, the first thing you need to determine is your reaction to the dream. I'm not just talking about how you feel; but, determine what spiritual force you are experiencing—your inner man. Where did your dream originate? Compile your own list of spiritual forces that come from God and those that come from Satan.

    GOD:

    _____

    SATAN:

DIRECTIVE DREAMS HELP US SEE FURTHER DOWN THE ROAD THAN WE PRESENTLY ARE AND HELP US AVOID MANY PITFALLS ALONG THE WAY OF FULFILLING DIVINE DESTINY.

DREAM SHARING

26. In the "Dreams about Teeth" section on page 90 of your text, I shared a very simple dream I had where I only saw two front teeth with braces. I immediately knew that it was wisdom that I needed. However, I didn't have peace that the interpretation was complete. After a few months, I finally understood the full message. What was the message the Lord was showing me? Why might God use this two-step method of dealing with us? Have you had any dreams where you have had a two-step interpretation?

27. We discussed the python spirit on page 100 of your text. Explore and share how this spirit tries to work against God's plans. Examine Acts 16:16 where the slave girl had an ungodly spirit of divination (python) to tell the future. What was Paul doing when the python spirit showed up? What was the goal of this spirit? Have you ever experienced this spirit's influence? How can you combat this demonic influence? Use Bible study tools to further your learning (www.BibleHub.com is a good source).

DREAM ANSWERS - LESSON 5

1. a) Yes; b) Prosperity, safety, hope, and a future (p 77-78).
2. Expected end (p 78).
3. God-given dreams to empower you to be your best (p 78).
4. Mysteries; heal (p 78).
5. You must drive out the previous occupants and actively go in to occupy your personal promised land through God's direction, which is given through dreams that guide you to your destiny. Pursue your promises from God (p 79).
6. Hope; life (p 79).
7. We must remember God's character and the way He operates (p 80).
8. Revelation; impartation (p 81).
9. Edify – dreams about building me up; exhort – dreams that stir me up and give me the courage and hope to press on; comfort – dreams that stir up faith for healing in my spirit, soul, and body (p 80-82).
10. God gives you this type of dream to prepare you for something new or to produce a change in your life (p 83).
11. Learn (p 83).
12. People present, what kind of school, subjects, etc. Are you continually taking the same test? Varies (p 84).
13. Your purpose, calling, ministry, or profession (p 84).
14. Nothing is always! (p 85).
15. Condemnation (p 80).
16. Motive, heart issues, pain, trauma, etc. (p 91).
17. Because nothing is always. This is our one golden rule.
18. Seek God to ensure you are accurately understanding His message at that moment.
19. God gives directive dreams to give you vision for the future—the long-game—and helps you sidestep any snares or dangers in your journey ahead (p 99).
20. Varies.
21. Varies. Examples include: 1) Storms–Future is being unveiled; 2) Flying–Rising above the problem; 3) Nakedness–Feeling exposed and vulnerable; 4) Teeth–Needing wisdom; 5) Bathrooms–Cleansing is needed. (p 83-101).
22. Varies. Examples include: "I tell myself I'm stupid;" " I tell myself it's my fault;" etc. (p 89).
23. Breath–Job 33:4; Comforter–Jer 8:18; Counselor–Jn 14:26, 15:26; Advocate–Jn 14:16; Convicts us of sin–Jude 1:15; Intercessor–He 7:25; Revealer–1 Cor 2:10; Spirit of Truth–Jn 16:13; Teacher–Lk 2:12. Varies. Example: "I really need the Holy Spirit as the Comforter right now because..." (p 80).
24. Varies. Example: "I can do all things through Christ" (Phil 4:13). "I am the head and not the tail" (Deut 28:13). etc (p 89).
25. Varies. God: hope, faith, encouragement, peace, comfort, etc. Satan: fear, discouragement, doubt, condemnation, etc. (p 79).
26. Varies. God showed me that I needed to brace myself about a coming situation that required wisdom. God might use a two-step interpretation because that is all we can "hear" at the time. Circumstances may need to align that would allow us to understand the interpretation in full (p 90).
27. A python spirit tries to rob you of your hopes and dreams; it wants to squeeze the life out of you. ***Strong's Concordance*** says python *(puthón)* is a masculine Greek noun whose meaning is "a divining spirit." In Acts 16:16, this spirit's goal was to distract Paul from prayer and his mission and subject him to persecution. To destroy a python spirit, you must know your spiritual authority and do what Paul and Silas did: worship God and pray. Don't give up; resist the devil, and he will flee (p 100).

DREAM JOURNALING

When interpreting dreams, you must think like a journalist by asking who, what, where, when, and how. These are the things that you will want to train yourself to be attentive to when you have a dream. Continue to practice your skills and take into account the destiny dreams that we covered in this chapter when you record your dream.

Dream 1:

Dream 2:

JOSEPH'S DREAMS PURIFIED HIS HEART AND MOTIVES; HE WAS BEING REFINED BY THE HAND OF GOD UNTIL HIS TIME CAME TO FULFILL HIS DREAMS.

LESSON 6

OTHER COMMON DESTINY DREAMS

DREAM TEXT

Everyone needs to develop his/her own intimate language with God. Even though I am providing lists of symbols that have proven helpful, we are never to depend on someone else's revelation. A person's dream language is private, personal and intimate. The Holy Spirit is our main teacher. Other teachers and instructors provide help, but eventually we must hear from the Lord ourselves! This is all part of our discovery and Spirit-led journey (*Understanding Your Dreams*, 106).

DREAM FOCUS

When interpreting your dreams, the most important thing is to understand what God is speaking to you. Utilize the tools you have been given and acquire some personal understanding, but the most important thing is to develop your own dream language to hear God's message to you. Don't allow yourself to fret over the interpretation. God understands you and your makeup; He will help you understand. Do your part through study and prayer; have faith that the Lord will do His part. He is faithful!!

DREAM THINKING

1.   ☐ True ☐ False   When interpreting dreams, it is most important to strictly adhere to current thought from dream scholars. Include a couple of sentences to support your answer.

REMEMBER:

"Nothing is always—most revelation from God is birthed out of intimacy, so the more time we spend with Him, the more He empowers us with greater understanding of our dreams!"
~ Sandie Freed

2. What are common thoughts that dreaming about a house could represent?
    _____, _____, or _____.

3. One of the most common types of dream involves your house. Analyze the bulleted items on pages 107-108 in your text and construct a user-friendly list of things you will want to pay attention to when having this dream. Include the reason why.

4. Sometimes dreams may expose things in your life, but the ultimate purpose is to _____.

5. _____ are messengers, and they always carry a _____.

6. What two questions did the Lord tell me to ask angels that would be helpful for you, too?

    1)_____

    2)_____

7. When you have a dying dream in black and white, it could possibly mean that it is _____ inspired.

8. A dream that evokes fear and torment probably originates from _____. List some Bible verses that support your answer.

RUN
to God
NOT
from God

9. What type of dream could a person with control issues possibly have? What are some Scriptures you could use to help get free of these control issues?

10. How can the devil influence your dreams?

11. Define natural dreaming.

12. According to Genesis 50:20, God takes what was meant for evil against you and turns it to good. God can also turn the terror and panic caused by nightmares to your good. How can He do this?

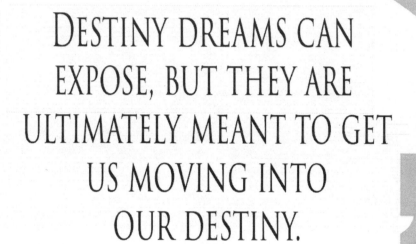

DESTINY DREAMS CAN EXPOSE, BUT THEY ARE ULTIMATELY MEANT TO GET US MOVING INTO OUR DESTINY.

13.   In this chapter, I discuss lucid dreaming. Explain what lucid dreaming is in your own words. How can you enforce your victory as a child of God when having a lucid dream?

14.   How do you know where your dream originates? Why would you need to know where a dream comes from?

DREAM APPLICATION

15.   On page 112 of your text, I talk about how a dying dream could possibly mean one of three things. In your words, list each one and include a sentence or two to expound on it.

1)

_____

2)

_____

3)

REMEMBER:

"Not all dreams are from God."
~ Sandie Freed

16. Dreams originate from three places. Explain what these are and how they work. What is the by-product of each type of dream?

    1)

    _____

    2)

    _____

    3)

DREAM ACTIVATION

17. Think about the evil-inspired dreams you have experienced personally: false dreams, dark dreams, some nightmares, lucid dreams, etc. How could God use these specifically for your good? If you are subject to this type of dream, how can you use anointing oil to help?

TRUST
in the
LORD
with all your
♥HEART
PROV 3:5

DREAM SHARING

18. Evil-inspired dreams can be used to rob you of refreshing sleep and steal your destiny. Think about nightmares you have had and what you can learn from them. Look up Bible verses that promise you good (sweet, pleasing, pleasant) sleep as a believer.

19. In a hypothetical dream, a married woman dreamed she had a baby. According to Chuck Pierce's dream types (p 105-106), what are the possible meanings of this dream?

    Simple Message:

    _____

    Simple Symbolic Dream:

DREAM ANSWERS - LESSON 6

1. False. You need to find your own dream language and seek God for understanding in each case. Nothing is always when you are interpreting dreams (p 105-106).
2. Your life, your church, or your mind (p 107).
3. Varies. House Repair–possibly symbolic that your life needs repair; rooms–each room can have different meanings: bedroom–intimacy with the Lord; bathroom–cleansing, etc. Localized worrisome events in your home–healing is coming (p 107-108).
4. To get us to move forward to our destiny in God (p 108).
5. Angels; message (p 109).
6. Ask the Lord: 1) Why did You send the angel? and 2) What message are they bringing? (p 109).
7. Demonically (p 112).
8. The devil or demons. Verses could include: 1 Jn 4:8; Ro 8:15; 1 Cor 16:10; Eph 6:20; Is 43:1; Deut 31:6-8; Phil 4:6-7; Ps 56:13; 2 Tim 1:7; Matt 6:25-34; Jos 1:9; 1 Pe 5:7; Ps 118:6; etc. (p 117).
9. A falling dream. Jer 29:11; Josh 1:9; Matt 6:34; Matt 19:26; Is 41:10; Ps 115:3; Matt 11:28-30; Ps 37:24; Jer 23:23-24; Deut 8:11; Prov 19:21; Phil 4:6-7, 13; 1 Pe 5:6-7; etc. Varies (p 113-114).
10. Satan can assail you with ideas, promptings, or suggestions which can be worrisome or distressful to you. These emotions can influence your dreams negatively (p 114).
11. Dreams that come through your soul—what you're thinking about, concerned about, watching on TV, listening to, etc. Dreams are a way for our human minds to sort out our daily thoughts and feelings. Dear one, we must be prayerful to determine the origin of our dreams (p 116).
12. Nightmares can inspire revelation in areas of your life that cause bondage and confusion. God can uncover the enemy and tactics that he is using against you (p 120).
13. Lucid dreaming is being aware that you are dreaming and possibly controlling parts of the dream. You can re-enter your dream and enforce your victory by taking authority over the influencing spirit and directing the outcome (p 120-121).
14. Ask the Holy Spirit to divulge the origin. Evaluate whether you have the peace of God. If you don't know the dream source immediately, pray and seek God; possibly obtain godly counsel for assistance. You need to know the origin of a dream to determine your actions: receive it, rebuke it, or ignore it (p 116-120).
15. 1) Depending on the person who dies, the dream may symbolically mean there will be an end to a season (career, ministry, job, etc.). 2) a colorful dying dream may indicate that something is going to be eliminated, but will be restored back to you with a great breakthrough. 3) It could be a literal dream—a call to intercession regarding another's health condition (p 112).
16.   1) God–can speak to you about things in the past, present, or things to come. These will usually be communicated through symbolism to protect the message that He has for you. By-product of this dream: joy, peace, comfort, etc. (p 79-83). 2) Satan–can influence your thoughts and dreams through his lies and false accusations. By-product of this dream: fear, anxiety, depression, etc. (p 117-120). 3) Natural Dreams–can originate from your human soul effected by your daily concerns, fears, etc. Dreams can also be influenced by drugs and what you watch on TV. By-product of this dream: varies (p 116-117).
17. Varies. God can use nightmares to expose hidden areas of your heart or fears; He can use it to show an area needing healing in order to move us forward. He can use a lucid dream to involve you in creating a victorious end. With anointing oil, you can anoint the mantle of your bedroom door and forbid the enemy's presence. Make the area out of bounds for the devil (p 117-121).
18. Varies. Examples: Prov 3:24; Ps 4:8; Ps 127:2; Job 11:19; Jer 31:26; Phil 4:7.
19. Simple message could be an encouragement that the woman was going to have a baby. The simple symbolic message could be that the dreamer is entering something new or possibly she is feeling helpless about an area (p 111).

Dream Journaling

Hopefully, by this time, you have asked the Lord to speak to you in dreams and visions and are in the habit of waking up to write down the details. Seek God regarding the origin of each dream and be alert to any symbols you may see. Continue to color and sketch throughout this study guide. You will also find it useful to study the verses listed in the answer sections along with the verses you find.

Dream 1:

Dream 2:

GOD ALWAYS INTENDS FOR DREAMS TO POINT US TO HIM & HIS WORD. WHEN DREAMS OCCUR, WE MUST BE LED BY THE SPIRIT OF GOD INTO EACH INTERPRETATION.

LESSON 7

UNDERSTANDING SYMBOLISM

DREAM TEXT

All through Scripture we can see that God speaks in symbolism. And because dreams are very often an expression of our own emotions, much symbolism is involved. As children of God, we are each on a journey to discover the interpretations of our dreams, first through Scripture and then from the backdrop of our own lives (*Understanding Your Dreams*, 123).

DREAM FOCUS

It is important for us to reflect on symbolism that you see in the Word. As you pay particular attention to God's established symbolism, you will begin to understand how He is speaking through your dreams. Become an expert in God's symbolic language, and then it's safe to add other godly resources to your arsenal.

DREAM THINKING

1.   What is the fundamental "law of first mention" of Bible study?

2.   Can the meaning of a dream symbol vary? Why? Yes ☐ No ☐

REMEMBER:

"the details of the dream before they are forgotten, and you will have most of what you need to interpret dreams."
~ Sandie Freed

3. What does the "law of first mention" have to do with dream interpretation?

4. What is the first tool to utilize in dream interpretation?

5. Keep the _____ thing the _____ thing.

6. Why is it important to establish the context of a dream?

7. A ☐ repeating or ☐ recurring dream is given because (1) you missed an element of understanding when you had the dream, (2) you misinterpreted the dream, or (3) your reaction to the dream was inadequate. Check one.

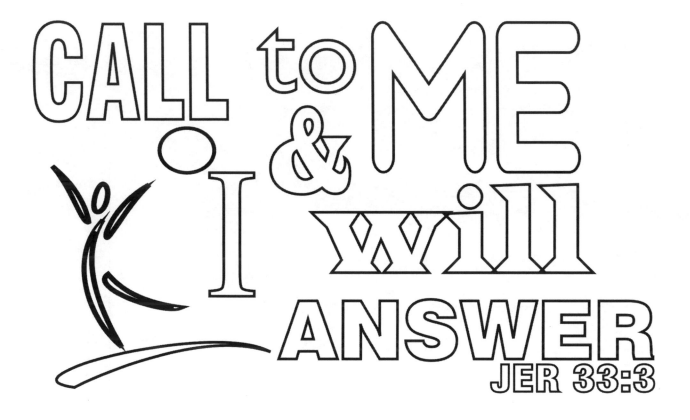

8.   What's the difference between a repeating and a recurring dream?

9.   If you have a dream where you are witnessing or watching the action rather than being the main person in the dream, it could mean that the dream is about _____ and you need to _____ for them.

10.   What are the two moments in time that you need to be aware of your emotions when interpreting dreams? Why are these emotions important?

      1)

      2)

11.   _____ is responsible for guiding your dream interpretations.

12.   ☐ True   ☐ False   God shows us dreams about others for us to go correct them.

13.   In Scripture, God often speaks _____ through parables and allegories.

14.   What is the first place you should consult when interpreting a dream?

> ARE YOU BEING ACCOUNTABLE TO GOD CONCERNING YOUR DREAMS? DO YOU WRITE DOWN YOUR DREAMS, PRAY OVER THEM, AND ASK GOD TO REVEAL THE INTERPRETATIONS?

15.   It can be _____ to rely on a single source to interpret dreams—including this book—with the exception of the Scriptures.

16.   ☐ True   ☐ False   A black and white dream is always demonic in origin. Why?

17.   Numbers are important to God, and He often uses them to communicate with us. As a general truth, what do the following numbers represent (you may need to consult the dictionary in chapter 9):

       3:
       _____

       6:
       _____

       7:
       _____

       8:
       _____

18.   ☐ True   ☐ False   The time on the clock that you awaken from having a dream may be important. Give the reason for your answer.

19.   In review, God gives you dreams and visions for _____, _____ and _____. Why does He do this?

REMEMBER:

"God at one time spoke through a donkey."
~ Sandie Freed

20. ☐ True ☐ False Once a dream is fully understood, it will come to pass immediately.

21. Why does God speak to us through the hidden meaning of dreams?

DREAM APPLICATION

22. List the seven (7) tools for dream interpretation and how they work (p 125-129). It would be wise to commit these tools to memory.

1)

2)

3)

4)

5)

6)

7)

23. Review the 17 thoughts regarding dream interpretation on pages 129-130 of your text. List four (4) items of which you need to continually remind yourself (try not to look at the text for this part).
1)

2)

3)

4)

"God desires to heal and restore us, and He uses dreams and visions to speak truth which will open the doors to our freedom. Jesus addressed this by sayng, 'Take heed how you hear.'"

24.   A stronghold is a fortified place or a place of bondage. What strongholds could a Christian have? How do you pull them down?

DREAM ACTIVATION

25.   The context of your dream symbol will direct the interpretation of your dream. In your text on page 126, I gave you the example of a lion. Let's analyze a hypothetical dream about a bird. Think about how birds are used in the Bible. How will dreams of different birds lead you to different meanings?

SEE IN PART
KNOW IN PART
BUT THEN FACE TO FACE

DREAM SHARING

26.   The more you learn about dreams, the more important it is to keep the three golden rules of dream interpretation in the forefront of your thinking in order to avoid the pitfalls of human error. Study these rules to understand them and to entrench them in your thinking. Share your thoughts of what each rule entails and why each is important.

   1) Nothing is always.

   2) Remember the character and nature of the Holy Spirit.

   3) Go to the Scriptures first (stick with biblical sources altogether and avoid psychoanalytical babble).

27.   Think about any areas of stronghold you may have or currently have in your life. Talk about the steps you have used to get free of strongholds or steps that you have studied about.

DREAM ANSWERS - LESSON 7

1. Study the 1st appearance of a word/symbol to gain understanding of its inherent meaning in other locations. This principle cannot be applied 100% of the time, but is a good springboard to discover what God is speaking to you (p 123-124).

2. Yes. Nothing is always. A symbol does not mean the same thing all the time; that is why we need interpretation to evaluate the context and specific meaning at that time (p 123).

3. The Lord will speak to you and utilize a pattern of symbols to build further communication with you. You will find as you gain understanding, the meaning behind certain symbols will remain the same. This will bring a confidence to your interpretation as you gain experience; however, always be available to gain a greater depth of understanding to various symbols (p 125).

4. KISS–keep it simple "sweetheart." Analyze your dream down to the main theme while ignoring all the non-essential details. Too many details can confuse the interpretation (p 125-126).

5. Main, main (p 126).

6. When you establish the proper context of a dream through prayerful observation, you can determine the course of the interpretation. It's imperative to establish the context—the setting, situation, circumstance of a dream (p 126).

7. Repeating (p 127).

8. A repeated dream is to emphasize a message, correct an understanding, or modify a response. A recurring dream occurs more than two times in a given period to settle a matter of unforgiveness, healing of wounds, etc. (p 126-127).

9. Someone else; pray (p 128).

10. 1) During the dream; 2) when you wake up after the dream. Emotions indicate something to be dealt with. Waking emotions may be an indicator of where the dream originated, i.e. if you feel joyful & peaceful when you wake up, it's probably a dream from the Lord; if you feel fear or panic, the dream could have an evil or natural origin (p 129).

11. The Holy Spirit (p 129).

12. False. God shows us dreams about others to intercede on their behalf—pray for them (p 128).

13. Symbolically (p 131).

14. The Bible (p 131).

15. Dangerous (p 131).

16. False. A black and white dream can be an indicator of evil-inspired dreams; however, prophetic dreams without color can be from God. Remember that colors are indicators, but it's the context of the dream that matters (p 132).

17. 3: the number of the Trinity; 6: the number of man; 7: perfection or completion; 8: new beginnings (p 135, 179).

18. True. God may be emphasizing a truth through the actual time. Record the times & you may note a pattern (p 133).

19. Edification, exhortation, comfort. God gives us uplifting dreams because He wants to inspire hope to finish the race. Sometimes He wants to reinforce our courage and confidence that we are pursuing His will (p 135).

20. False. Dreams are not on our timetable; it takes faith and patience to inherit promises. It also takes worship and prayer to ensure God's results (p 135).

21. God often grants dreams in order to speak straight to your spirit and circumvent your intellect. Sometimes you may not have an "ear to hear," or you may need to build your faith, but He drops a hint of His message or correction into your spirit to prepare you (p 137).

22. 1) KISS–simplicity; 2) Context–what is the symbol doing?; 3) Recurring dream–have you had this dream before?; 4) Full picture–are you an observer or a main actor?; 5) Role–what are you doing in the dream?; 6) Focus–is the dream centered around you? Where were you?; 7) Emotions–what emotions are stirred during and after the dream? (p 125-129).

23. See the list on pages 129-130.

24. Varies. Greed, envy, lust, jealousy, covetousness, addiction, etc. Pulling down strongholds is a spiritual battle where you take authority & render the enemy powerless & ineffective in your life. Continue to build your faith and renew your minds to the Word to take thoughts captive. Consult your pastor or spiritual leader if you need help (p 127, 134).

25. Varies. Dove=peace, comfort, gentleness. Eagle=strength, a seer (prophet), soaring. Vulture=flesh, uncleanness (p 126).

26. Varies.

27. Varies. See question 24. Also, use the armor of God (2 Cor 10:4; Eph 6:10-18) to tear down strongholds.

DREAM JOURNALING

Continue to ask God to speak to you through dreams and visions. Have faith in your prayer because He has promised to speak to us in the last days. Pay attention to colors, numbers, feelings, and any symbols that show up in your dreams. Continue to seek God regarding the message. Remember that dreams from God will edify, exhort, and comfort you. Look up all the Bible verses in the answer section for a more intense study.

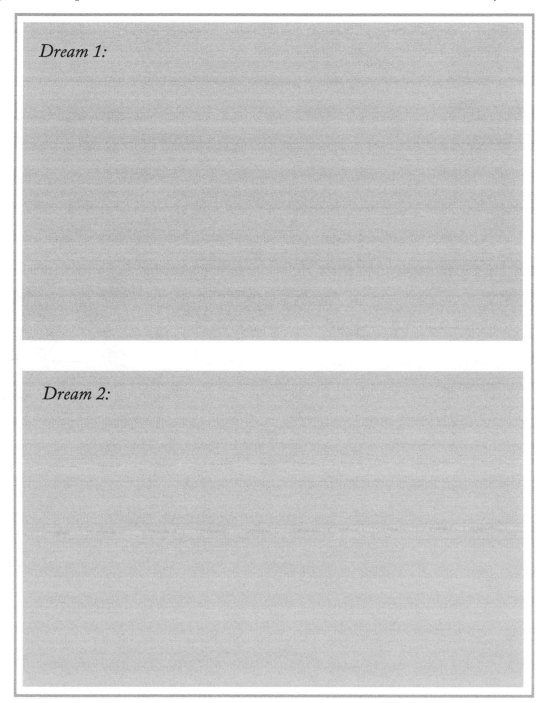

Dream 1:

Dream 2:

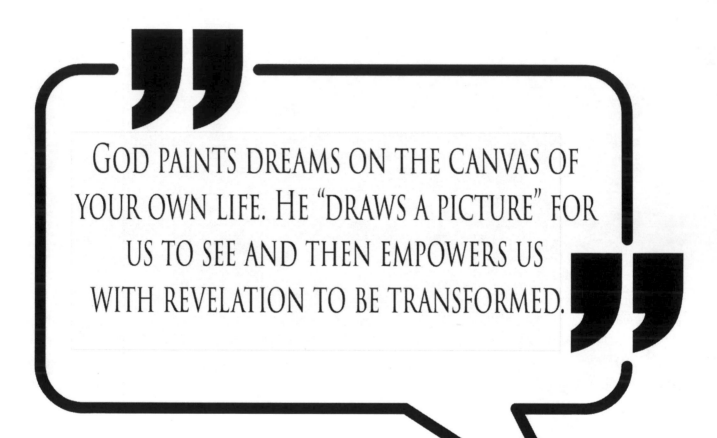

GOD PAINTS DREAMS ON THE CANVAS OF YOUR OWN LIFE. HE "DRAWS A PICTURE" FOR US TO SEE AND THEN EMPOWERS US WITH REVELATION TO BE TRANSFORMED.

LESSON 8

APPLYING INTERPRETATION

DREAM TEXT

Dreams are a universal language—there are dreamers all over the world from all nations and cultures...We must never assume, however, that even universal symbolism always represents the same thing in every dream...The symbol depends completely on the dreamer's understanding and personal dream vocabulary (*Understanding Your Dreams*, 142).

DREAM FOCUS

The most important thing for you when interpreting dreams is to: record your dream, pray, and seek God for the interpretation. Following that, you may need to search the Bible for wisdom to unlock the symbolism in your dream. Books on dreams may possibly help you hear God's message. You will need to develop some skills to establish your foundational dream vocabulary. Then practice, practice, practice.

DREAM THINKING

1.   How is learning God's heavenly dream language like learning a foreign language?

2.   God's dream language becomes native to us through _____, _____, _____, and _____.

REMEMBER:

"We must always use discernment when interpreting dreams."
~ Sandie Freed

3. Jesus spoke in parables and symbols throughout His ministry. In Matthew 16:5-12, He spoke of the Pharisee's leaven. What did the disciples think He meant? What was He referring to with this symbol?

4. Symbols alluding to Jesus are many. Some of them include: _____, _____, _____, _____, and _____.

5. An image that stands for something is a _____.

6. ☐ True   ☐ False   Symbols in a dream have significance.

7. Discuss this statement: Dreams are a universal language. Why could that be a mistaken assumption? What is one universal symbol that rarely changes?

8. The symbolic interpretation of any dream depends on two things. What are they?

    1)_____

    2)_____

9. ☐ True   ☐ False   When interpreting a dream, always assume that unknown people and places mean nothing in your dream.

10. What could God be showing you when you feel emotions in your dreams? Why would He show you this?

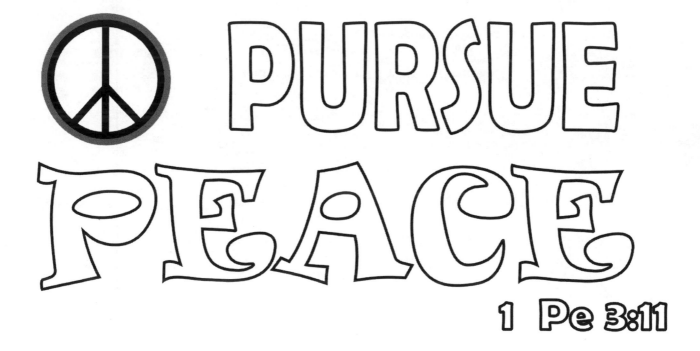

11. Symbolic meanings are not always logical deductions and interpretations; dreams must be _____ understood.

12. Explain how the proper interpretation belongs to the dreamer.

13. How can you be misled by utilizing dream books to give the sole interpretation of a dream? What is the purpose of any dream book or dictionary?

14. Discuss the interpretation possibilities for a snake dream.

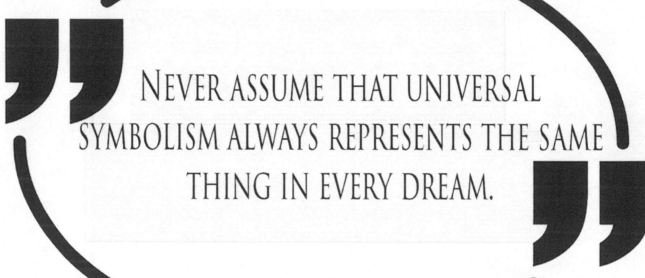

NEVER ASSUME THAT UNIVERSAL SYMBOLISM ALWAYS REPRESENTS THE SAME THING IN EVERY DREAM.

15. You must always use spiritual _____ when interpreting dreams accurately.

16. What is the "inner witness"? Why is this important when interpreting dreams?

17. What is meant by dream confirmation? What are other methods of confirming a dream?

18. When receiving a confirmed word from the Lord in a vision or dream, it is important for you to _____.

19. Why is it important to continue asking God for His gifts?

REMEMBER:

"If you are not the main subject, you are basically an observer. The dream, therefore, is not directly about you. This is a dream that is usually meant for prayer."
~ Sandie Freed

20. What is the #1 response to a dream you have?

21. When you are not the main person in your dream, the dream is usually meant for _____.

22. Why should you submit significant dreams to those in spiritual authority over you?

23. As in prophecy, a God-given dream is a message from Him. Dreams could be called "_____ while you sleep."

24. You should _____ try to make your dream come to pass; you must be patient and allow God to do things in His time.

25. ☐ True ☐ False   All God-given dreams will line up with the Bible.

PRECEPT UPON PRECEPT

LINE UPON LINE

Is 28:10

DREAM APPLICATION

26.   List the possible responses to your God-given dream:

        1)_____

        2)_____

        3)_____

        4)_____

27.   Why would you think it important for God to build your private dream
        vocabulary?

DREAM ACTIVATION

28.   Continue to pray and ask God to give you dreams and wake you up after them.
        What are the different ways to document your dreams that we discussed in the
        text? Which method do you think will work for you?

29.   You will not have any dreams to interpret if you can't recall them. What system
        can you put in place to help you wake up and recall your dreams?

> # MEANINGS FROM SYMBOLS DO NOT EMERGE BY COMING TO RATIONAL CONCLUSIONS, AND THEY ARE TO BE INDIVIDUALLY INTERPRETED.

Dream Sharing

30.   In Revelation 12, we see a woman giving birth with a dragon ready to devour her newborn. Read this chapter to discover the symbology. There are several interpretations for this chapter. In your text, I offer one interpretation; study your dream dictionary and other sources to gain revelation. Share the interpretation that God speaks to you.

31.   What method have you used to document your dreams? Has this worked for you? What advice could you share with others about this method?

32.   What is the most challenging thing about dream interpretation that you have experienced? What did you do to overcome this?

DREAM ANSWERS - LESSON 8

1. It is like learning a foreign language in that it doesn't always feel comfortable or right at first. Can be difficult to enunciate or hear properly. The symbols God uses may appear foreign (p 139-140).
2. Time/ effort/ discernment/ prayer (p 140).
3. They thought He meant the Pharisee's bread; however, He really meant their deceptive doctrines (p 140).
4. Vine/ door/ shepherd/ bread/ wine, etc. (p 140).
5. Symbol (p 141).
6. True (p 141).
7. Many symbols are recognized worldwide; however, seek the Lord for meaning. You also want to be mindful of the dreamer's specifics—personal dream language, personal understanding, etc. Ex: cross and smiley face (p 142, 144).
8. 1) Dreamer's understanding; 2) dreamer's personal dream vocabulary (p 142).
9. False. God may be trying to speak to you with the symbolic presence of these people or places. The more we become skillful at understanding God's use of these things, the more He can speak to us through them (p 143).
10. God may be showing you feelings you are experiencing daily in order to deal with any repressed emotions through spiritual healing or medical means (p 143).
11. Individually (p 144).
12. Only the dreamer understands the symbols in a dream. Dreams are relational—it's all about how symbols and events relate to the dreamer. Without prayer and possibly a divine gift, no one can interpret another's dreams (p 144).
13. Nothing is always; make no assumptions about a dream. You can be deceived if you make a straight-line book interpretation of a dream. Use dream books as a guide (p 145).
14. Snake=evil, but it can represent healing (medical caduceus). Also represents a curse (p 145).
15. Discernment (p 146).
16. God's Spirit speaks to our spirit; "inner witness" that links us up to God. Follow it, and you will avoid error and find peace. As the Psalmist said, "Seek peace and pursue it" (Ps 34:14) (p 146-147).
17. Confirmation agrees with your inner man. It is a divine aptitude that presses into God to ascertain a dream's meaning. Methods include: another dream, God's audible voice, visions, mental images, and the counsel of ministry (p 146).
18. Respond (p 147).
19. It is important to ask God for His gifts in faith believing He will impart them to you. Asking daily keeps your faith active and your expectations high. Be sure to thank Him for them, too (p 147)!
20. The #1 response to a God-given dream is wake up and write. Without recording the event, you leave the message to memory. In the middle of the night, you may or may not remember it (p 148, 150).
21. Prayer. Ask God how to pray about the message and persons in your dream (p 149).
22. You should submit significant dreams to your spiritual authority in humility—especially if the dream is about the church or church member. Pastors will be privy to information you don't have. Believe that God will use them in determining the dream's message. It's important to keep a humble attitude and have an ear to hear what your leaders say (p 150).
23. Prophecy (p 151).
24. NOT (p 151).
25. True (p 151).
26. 1) Write your dream when you awaken; 2) Stay open and teachable; 3) Honor the dream's interpretation; 4) Search the Scripture to ensure the message does not contradict the Word (p 147-152).
27. One reason is because a thing/event will mean something different to different people; God speaks within those confines. Varies (p 152).
28. Record a short synopsis of your dream; outline it; draw it; summarize main characters; etc. Varies (p 148-149).
29. Varies. Keep a specific means bedside to record your dreams. Possibly use a flashlight. Write. Return to sleep.
30. Woman=church; dragon=Antichrist. Interpretation=birth of the church with Antichrist spirit trying to abort the seed of God. Varies.　　31. Varies.　　32. Varies.

Dream Journal

Date: _____ Time: _____ Recurring? _____ If so, when? _____

Dream Title: _____

Main Character: ⬤ Self   ⬤ Other: _____

Your Role: ⬤ Participant   ⬤ Observer

Colors: ⬤ B&W   ⬤ Vivid   ⬤ Muted   Color/s: _____

Location: _____

What's in the Background? _____

Emotions During the Dream:	Emotions Upon Awakening:
⬤ Fear ⬤ Dread	⬤ Fear ⬤ Dread
⬤ Joy ⬤ Excitement	⬤ Joy ⬤ Excitement
⬤ Other _____	⬤ Other _____

What's the Dream About?

List or Sketch Important Symbols

Pray for the Interpretation

REMEMBER:

"Ask God first concerning the meaning of the symbolism in your dreams. Always let the Holy Spirit be your filter."
~ Sandie Freed

LESSON 9

A-Z DICTIONARY
OF SYMBOLISM

DREAM TEXT

As you have learned, dreams and visions are the major ways God speaks to us; therefore, it is wisdom to study the symbols within our dreams and visions so that we can properly respond to His voice. While it is true, as you have also learned, that not all dreams are from God, you will find that once you understand how He speaks in symbolism, you will be better equipped to discern the source of the dream (*Understanding Your Dreams*, 153).

DREAM FOCUS

I have included a symbolism dictionary in your text which is to serve as a general guide for you to use. The most important thing to remember is that you must always consult the Lord for any dream interpretations. This A-Z Dictionary will help you, but your personal dream language vocabulary will dictate an accurate understanding of your dream. Continue to develop your own vocabulary and practice with the dictionary.

DREAM THINKING

1.   The role of the Master Potter is to _____ and _____ us into God's _____ image.

2.   The filter you use for any dream interpretation should always be the _____. Why?

I WAS RAISED TO
BELIEVE THAT GOD DOES
NOT SPEAK THROUGH
DREAMS. I'M SO BLESSED
THAT I KNOW DIFFERENTLY
TODAY.

3.   When using this dream symbol dictionary, be sure to remember the following:

1)_____

2)_____

3)_____

4)_____

4.   Why would I say not to totally depend on this great A-Z Dictionary in your text?

5.   Why do some symbols in the dictionary have positive and negative aspects?

He will guide you into all truth

Jn 16:13

6.   What are the questions you should ask yourself when interpreting symbols?

1)_____

2)_____

3)_____

4)_____

DREAM APPLICATION

7.   ☐ True   ☐ False   A dream with a dog in it always represents a pet. Why or why not?

8.   What would a dream about a thief possibly mean? What Bible verse comes to mind?

9.   Many people have dreams about falling. What could this possibly mean?

REMEMBER:

"The Lord desires to build your own personal dream vocabulary!"
~ Sandie Freed

10. Imagine that a fictitious man praying for God's will had the following dream. Without knowledge of the man's personal dream vocabulary, you can only theorize what this dream could mean; include your theory below.

> *I was on a moving train. I had several school textbooks in my hands —they were my books. I awoke with questions about what the dream symbolized.*

11. Discuss the meaning of the number seven (7). Give three examples of the number seven being used in the Bible.

    1)_____

    2)_____

    3)_____

12. Here is another dream to analyze. Write out your observations. Imagine the dreamer is a young minister.

> *I was in a car driving along the mountainside. The weather was stormy and rainy. I was afraid during the dream when I thought I would drive off the cliff, and I was afraid when I woke up.*

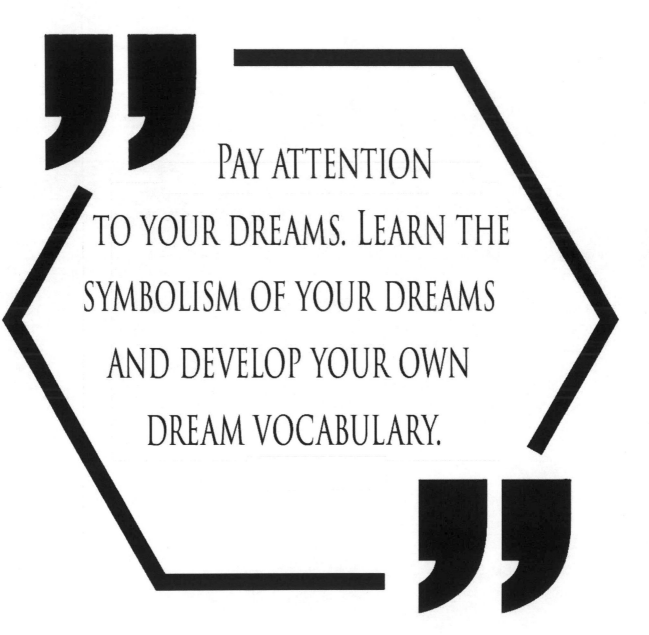

PAY ATTENTION TO YOUR DREAMS. LEARN THE SYMBOLISM OF YOUR DREAMS AND DEVELOP YOUR OWN DREAM VOCABULARY.

13.   If you dream about a hotel, you could be a person in _____.

14.   A young single woman keeps dreaming about committing adultery with an unknown person. What could this indicate? How would you advise her in the way to freedom?

15.   A boy continued to dream of a cupid who had a nest in a cemetery. The cupid would visit the child's house in the dream. The child would wake up terrified and try to scream out, but couldn't. His mother was actually buried in that same cemetery. What could this possibly mean?

DAN 7:1

DREAM ACTIVATION

16. Continually ask God to speak to you through dreams and visions. You will need to seek Him to hear His message. A dream given to you is a message to you, and He will give you understanding over time IF you seek Him. Remind yourself of God's use of dreams through the Bible and make note of those verses below. Choose verses that will specifically build your faith to receive God's special message to you. Recite these verses to yourself on a regular basis; you may want to include the list on your phone or small cards for easy use during the day.

17. Compare the blue car in these two dream versions:

    A man was driving a blue car and kept looking up at the trees while driving. He parked the car at a new home he was not familiar with, but it was his home.

    The second version is a man was driving a blue car and kept looking down at his speedometer worried about his speed. He parked his car at an unfamiliar house and began to wash his car.

18. If you had the dream below, what would you do with it?

    You see an unfamiliar woman enter a dark room and close the door. You see your pastor dressed in a brown suit (that you have never seen before). The pastor goes into the same dark room, but keeps his hand on the door knob.

> THE DEVIL DOES NOT WANT US TO POSSESS OUR PROMISED LAND! IF HE CAN SEDUCE US INTO APOSTASY, CONVINCING US TO REMAIN LUKEWARM, HE WILL STEAL OUR DESTINY!

DREAM SHARING

19.   Evaluate this dream and discuss what the symbols may represent and what the meaning of the dream could be. Of course, you won't know the exact meaning since the dreamer's understanding and dream language would determine that:

> *There was a huge rattlesnake, white with red diamonds, in our family room. We had an infant; I was shocked when I saw the baby walking with head phones over its ears. The baby went into room with snake, and I followed and saw a smaller rattlesnake at the entrance behind a blue sofa. My husband reached behind the sofa and had a terrible grimace from the pain. I knew he was bitten so I called 911. The ambulance was taking too long; I was frustrated that it took so long for us to leave. I realized the small snake was still loose so I rolled up a blue towel and hit the snake. Unbeknownst to me, the snake attached to the towel I was holding and something raked across my toe. I yelled out, "I think it bit me too." My aunt threw the snake out the door after I opened it. I awakened without notable emotions.*

20.   Are you experiencing more dreams? How confident are you in understanding your dreams? Are you being patient to seek God for the interpretation?

DREAM ANSWERS - LESSON 9

1. Mold; fashion; divine (p 153).
2. Holy Spirit (p 153). The Holy Spirit should be your filter because He knows all things, and He is eternal truth. He will help you weigh an interpretation in light of the Word and the character and nature of God.
3. 1) The list is a general guide; 2) it is not all-inclusive; 3) never totally depend on a list; 4) nothing is always (p 153-154).
4. The dictionary is just a tool—a guide to possibly understand what God is saying. You must listen to God as you seek the interpretation since the dream will be dependent on your personal dream vocabulary. The dictionary will help acquaint you with how God has spoken through symbolism to others (p 154).
5. Sometimes God may use a symbol positively or negatively. Emotions felt throughout a dream or when you wake up can direct you toward the positive or negative interpretation (p 154).
6. 1) Feelings in the dream, 2) peace or fear, 3) colors, 4) participant or observer (p 154).
7. False. A dog may represent a pet or terror/grief depending on your experience. Your inner witness will lead you to the correct interpretation (p 154).
8. Thief=Satan or possibly the loss of something. Consult the Bible for revelation about your dream. John 10:10 may come to mind, "The thief comes only to steal and kill and destroy..." Varies (p 190).
9. It could indicate a loss of control in your life. Waking up immediately following the dream could indicate God speaking something of importance that needs to be heard (p 168).
10. The moving train could symbolize transition or moving to a new place or progress toward something. The books could symbolize a need to go learn something—maybe even go to school. The fact that the books were school books could indicate a teaching anointing or a call to teach. Varies.
11. The number 7 indicates wholeness, perfection, or completeness. The definition could come from 7 days in a week—the end or completed week. Also, 7 stems on the lampstand could indicate that the covenant is complete. Naaman had to bathe in the River Jordan seven times to be clean or perfected (2 Kings 5:10). Jesus told Peter to forgive "seventy times seven" which could indicate a completeness to that forgiveness (Mt 18:22). Seven seals to God's judgment could indicate a complete judgment (Rev 5:1). Varies.
12. The dreamer's ministry/anointing could be undergoing a spiritual attack. The dream itself may be part of the spiritual attack since he was afraid upon awakening. Varies.
13. Transition (p 172).
14. The woman could be in spiritual adultery—placing something in her life above God. I would advise this woman to make sure she was free of unclean thoughts and actions regarding sexual purity. Secondly, I would ask her if she knew of anything that may be superseding God's Lordship. Thirdly, I would lead her in a prayer of repentance and asking God to reveal the area. Finally, I would advise her not to quit seeking the Lord until she had an answer and sensed total freedom (p 155).
15. The terror experienced by the child indicates the origin of the dream is demonic. It seems to be an attack on the child's family and the child. It could be an angel of light sent with an assignment against that child (p 214). Varies.
16. Dan 1:17, 2:19, 22 & 28; Joel 2:28; Acts 2:17; Deut 29:29; Lk 8:17; Jer 33:3. Varies.
17. V1: Man about to receive new revelation. V2: Similar, but blue car could be spirit of depression/anxiety (p 164). Varies.
18. First, pray for your pastor! Could be he's under spiritual attack of his flesh (brown suit). Woman could be seductress to draw pastor away— physically or spiritually. Could ask God if it was a warning or exposure of sin; however, the character of God would not expose a spiritual leader to a church member. If you are an intercessor, it could be a warning about coming attack. Best thing would be to submit dream to your pastor. Let God lead pastor on interpretation. However, continue praying. Satan goes about seeking whom he may devour; don't let your pastor be devoured (p 165, 128). Varies.
19. Possible interpretation: white snake=religious spirit; two snakes=disunity; baby=a new thing; head phones=could represents an inability to hear; blue appears 2 times in this dream (sofa and towel)=anxiety; aunt=family. Possible meaning: This family had generations of religious spirits which cause disunity, anxiety, and frustration. The youth need to be protected against this spirit. There had to be husband/wife unity to get rid of it. Varies.
20. Varies.

D r e a m   J o u r n a l

Date: _____ Time: _____ Recurring? _____ If so, when? _____

Dream Title: _____

Main Character: ◯ Self   ◯ Other: _____

Your Role: ◯ Participant   ◯ Observer

Colors: ◯ B&W   ◯ Vivid   ◯ Muted   Color/s: _____

Location: _____

What's in the Background? _____

Emotions During the Dream:
◯ Fear   ◯ Dread
◯ Joy   ◯ Excitement
◯ Other _____

Emotions Upon Awakening:
◯ Fear   ◯ Dread
◯ Joy   ◯ Excitement
◯ Other _____

What's the Dream About?

List or Sketch Important Symbols

Pray for the Interpretation

REMEMBER:

"It is a privilege to search out hidden meanings. He wants to draw you near and speak hidden mysteries to you. He desires to share His world with you."
~ Sandie Freed

LESSON 10

THE DREAM THAT SAVED MY LIFE

DREAM TEXT

For years I had wasted away under a death curse, a slow attempt at suicide. Now, supernaturally, the breath of hope and life filled me. I knew I could survive this devastating bout with anorexia and bulimia, for God had spoken to me through my daughter. For the first time, I heard His voice through a dream (*Understanding Your Dreams*, 200).

DREAM FOCUS

As the chapter title suggests, I share about the life-changing dream that God used to save my life. Almighty God spoke to my young daughter in a dream to inspire me to live and not die. He got my attention! The choice to live is not always easy; the devil likes to keep you hooked and keep you feeling defeated. We must awaken to God's promise of abundant life and freedom in every area of our lives. Don't settle for less than total freedom! I like to share about freedom because I was so bound by the enemy. This chapter is designed to offer hope to the hopeless and peace to the restless.

DREAM THINKING

1. Who appeared in my daughter's dream and warned of my impending death? Why?

2. To understand the fullness of the word "deliverance," let's look at the Hebrew word which means _____ and the Greek word for "deliverance" which translates out to _____.

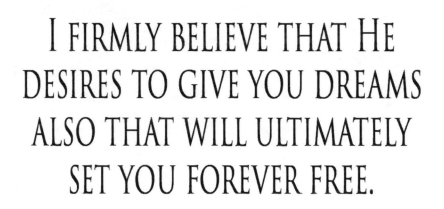

I FIRMLY BELIEVE THAT HE DESIRES TO GIVE YOU DREAMS ALSO THAT WILL ULTIMATELY SET YOU FOREVER FREE.

3.   What do dreams have to do with deliverance?

4.   What does it mean to say, "God is back from the future"?

5.   Dreams are often _____ that you need for your freedom.

6.   As you continue to read your text and work through this Study Guide, I am believing for you to have a tangible divine impartation to experience all _____.

7.   Let's review by you defining a stronghold. Do you have any strongholds? Take time now to re-examine your life and ask God to bring up any area where you need freedom from a long-standing hold on your life.

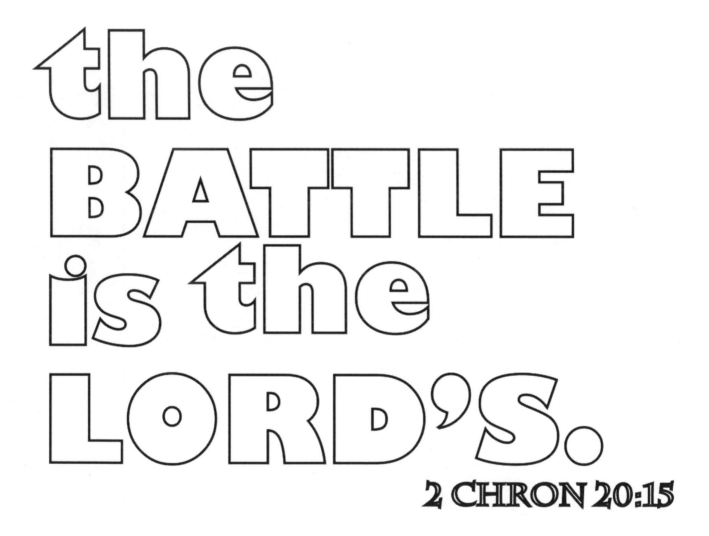

DREAM APPLICATION

8.   Read Luke 4:18 in three other translations (www.BibleHub.com has great parallel Bible translations). Fill in the blanks below and the translations you choose to help you meditate on this verse. Which version best speaks to you?

KJV   :to preach deliverance to the captives, to set at liberty them that are bruised

_____ :to _____ , to _____

_____ :to _____ , to _____

_____ :to _____ , to _____

9.   List some areas of freedom that you have found in Christ or list some areas shown in the Bible and a reference verse.

REMEMBER:

"We must exercise spiritual discernment when receiving and interpreting dreams and visions."
~ Sandie Freed

DREAM ACTIVATION

10. God wants you whole and walking in freedom. Can you think of any area in your life where you need deliverance, freedom, or a pardon for some past/present sin? If you're unsure, take time to ask God to reveal any areas to you. Pray the prayer of repentance and RECEIVE God's forgiveness. If this is an area where Satan continues to hound you, you're not free yet; seek God about the root of this sin. Once the root is exposed, you will be able to take authority over it and cast it out of your life. Write down Scriptures regarding your battle and coming victory.

11. Secret sins are not hidden from God. Be brave to get free of any hidden bondage in your life. There are some areas in my life that required help from a professional counselor; don't be afraid to reach out to your pastor or a counselor for strongholds that keep you from walking in complete victory. For your own use, note any sins that you are ashamed of or hide. What Bible verses can help you?

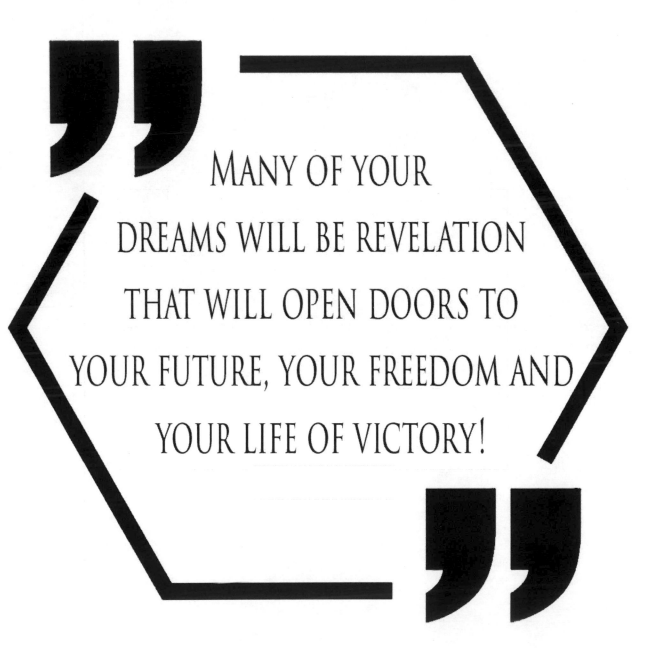

"MANY OF YOUR DREAMS WILL BE REVELATION THAT WILL OPEN DOORS TO YOUR FUTURE, YOUR FREEDOM AND YOUR LIFE OF VICTORY!"

DREAM SHARING

12. I shared the dream that saved my life—the interesting thing is that it was not my dream; it was given to my daughter for me. Revisit any time when you had a dream or someone else shared a dream with you that was a monumental experience in your life.

13. Have you ever chosen not to share a dream with someone when the dream was about them? Have you had a dream about another that you shared with them? In hindsight, did you do the right thing? How would you decide whether to share it or not?

DREAM ANSWERS - LESSON 10

1. Jesus, "the man in the sky." He appeared in order to get my attention. I wouldn't live for myself, but I would live for my precious baby girl (p 199).

2. Hebrew = to rescue; Greek = freedom and pardon or forgiveness, liberty, and remission; varies. (p 201).

3. Dreams often contain divine insight or revelation that show where you are in bondage or possibly the root of sin in your life. The first step of freedom is to realize you are in bondage. Your God-given dream may be the key to your freedom (p 201-202).

4. When I say this, I mean that your dream may contain in it revealed knowledge that will open up your future to a victorious life. God is omnipresent—He is in your past, present, and future at the same time. He knows the beginning from the end. He knows the mistakes you have made, and He sees your future deliverance through the blood of Jesus Christ. God sees you complete and whole. You have the victory now; choose to walk in it (p 202).

5. Revelation (p 202).

6. Heaven has to offer (p 202).

7. A stronghold is a reinforced and fortified demonic position of influence in our lives. It may be caused by our own decisions, experiences, or something from our ancestry. Varies.

8. Varies (p 201).

9. Freedom from sin (Ro 6:18); freedom from death (Ro 8:2); freedom from sickness (Ro 8:11); freedom from darkness (Col 1:13-14); freedom from oppression (Lk 4:18-19); freedom from wrath (Jn 3:36); freedom from dead works (He 9:14); freedom from temptation (2 Pe 2:9, KJV). Varies (p 203-205).

10. With God all things are possible (Matt 19:26). If the Son sets you free, you are free indeed (Jn 8:36). If God be for me, who can be against me (Ro 8:31). He has given me authority over all the enemy (Lk 10:19). Thanks be to God who has given me the victory (1 Cor 15:57). Victory rests with the Lord (Prov 21:31). The battle is the Lord's (2 Chron 20:15). The book of Psalms has many verses about victory. Varies.

11. Varies.

12. Varies.

13. Varies. You can decide whether to share a dream with the person you dreamed about based on the leading of the Holy Spirit. Ask the Lord what you should do. Remember, the other person may only be symbolic of something in your life. If you sense it's a God-dream that is important, you might consider sharing it with your pastor or spiritual leader for guidance.

D r e a m   J o u r n a l

Date: _____ Time: _____ Recurring? _____ If so, when? _____

Dream Title: _____

Main Character: ○ Self ○ Other: _____

Your Role: ○ Participant ○ Observer

Colors: ○ B&W ○ Vivid ○ Muted Color/s: _____

Location: _____

What's in the Background? _____

Emotions During the Dream:
○ Fear ○ Dread
○ Joy ○ Excitement
○ Other _____

Emotions Upon Awakening:
○ Fear ○ Dread
○ Joy ○ Excitement
○ Other _____

What's the Dream About?

List or Sketch Important Symbols

Pray for the Interpretation

REMEMBER:

"Because of the cross Satan has already been defeated. Like the Israelites, however, we must still use our spiritual authority to drive the enemy out of our Promised Land."
~ Sandie Freed

LESSON 11

DELIVERANCE THROUGH DREAMS

DREAM TEXT

When you declare God's Word and speak forth His promises concerning your life and future, you are cutting off the voice of the enemy. Yes! When you decree your promises, you cut down the enemy; you cut off his plans and you exclude yourself from them. Isn't that awesome? (*Understanding Your Dreams*, 210).

DREAM FOCUS

In this chapter, I shared with you a supernatural event that broke through my walls where everything suddenly became real to me. The door opened for me to hear God tell me to change my behavior NOW or I would die. In that moment, I had the victory I had long-sought after; I chose life. Throughout my life, dreams and visions have been tied to my deliverance. This is why I'm so passionate about sharing this truth and my testimony with you. Deliverance is yours—it may be a huge issue or it may be a small annoying issue; but, saint, it's yours to choose to walk in God's victory and freedom.

DREAM THINKING

1. In John 8:32, 36, the Bible says that KNOWLEDGE of the truth will make you free. What truth is being referenced here? What is the key to make this work?

2.   Freedom is available to all Christians, but why are we not all walking in freedom?

3.   We walk free from demonic influence by _____, _____, and _____ with Bible truths.

4.   ☐ True   ☐ False   If you fail to receive the dreams and visions God gives you, you are in fact rejecting truth.

5.   How will the Body of Christ benefit by accepting God-given dreams and visions?

6.   According to Hebrews 5:14 (KJV), we become of "full age" when we are _____ and put away _____ things.

7.   Do you understand what "strong meat" is in Hebrews 5:14 (KJV)? Explain your thoughts.

> "My life, my hope, my strength were in the anointing of God. As long as I was flowing and moving in that, the devil had no place in my life."

8.   A huge danger for Christians is to _____ with Satan's
_____.

9.   God is actively pursuing restoration for His saints. Examine the word "restore"
and write a definition in your own words.

10.   God has placed a potential or calling in you that is activated by
_____.

11.   Think about God's restoration. What is a benefit of restoration for God's people?

12.   In my story, I found some degree of freedom. At one point, I knew I needed
deliverance from the stronghold of anorexia; however, I didn't know anything
about deliverance. What indicated to me that I needed something more?

13. What is the difference between experiencing *chronos* time and *kairos* time? Which experience do we need to have a life-changing moment? Is there anything you can do to arrange for a *kairos* moment?

DREAM APPLICATION

14. I shared with you that God began to reconstruct defensive walls against fear, doubt, unbelief, insecurity, and abandonment in my life. As God rebuilds walls in your life, what defensive walls are you prayerful that He will rebuild for you?

15. Are there any areas where you need help—where you are pulled or controlled in some area of your life? It may not be sin; it may just be bondage. Ask God to reveal any bondages to you. What can you do about it?

REMEMBER:

"God is in control. And He will be faithful to guide you in the full revelation of your dreams."
~ Sandie Freed

16. After reading my testimony in this chapter about how God gave me a heavenly vision—a *kairos* moment—that brought deliverance to me, do you believe that everything is suddenly perfect in your life after such an experience?

17. Renewing your mind to the Word of God is essential in having the mind of Christ. However, there is a point where you decree or declare something in the spiritual realm to cut off Satan's voice in your life. Review the definition of "decree" on page 210 of your text. Make a list of decrees for YOU to speak to the mountain of demonic oppression to walk in freedom. Meditate on Matthew 17:14-20 and Job 22:28 in various translations.

WHEN YOU DECLARE GOD'S WORD AND SPEAK FORTH HIS PROMISES CONCERNING YOUR LIFE & FUTURE, YOU ARE CUTTING OFF THE VOICE OF THE ENEMY.

DREAM ACTIVATION

18.   Colossians 2:10 tells us that we are complete in Jesus. Do you feel like you are walking in that completeness? Are there areas in your life where you feel incomplete or unrestored? Examine these areas and look up Scriptures to help build your faith of God's promised completeness.

19.   In your quiet time, take your list of victorious decrees that you made in question 17 and cry out to God. Declare your victory in Christ. Declare your freedom in Jesus. Activate these promises in your life so that you can live out *sozo* or salvation in God (p 69, 147, 210). Speak to your mountain!

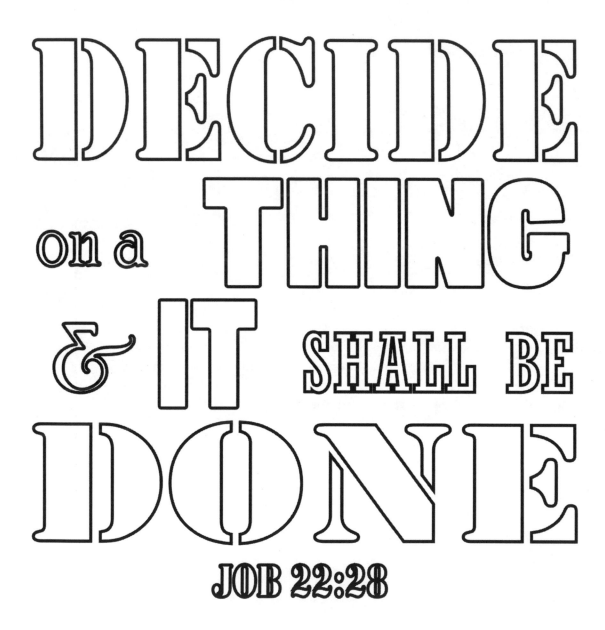

DECIDE on a THING & IT SHALL BE DONE

JOB 22:28

Dream Sharing

20.   Can you think back to any *kairos* moments that you have had in your life? Share some of these moments (p 206-207).

21.   Review my merry-go-round dream on pages 208-209 in your text. Have you ever felt like your spiritual life was on a merry-go-round? Think through some of those moments. What can you do to get off the merry-go-round once and for all? Share things you have done to receive your victory or things you will do.

DREAM ANSWERS - LESSON 11

1. The Word of God is truth. The key is knowledge of the Bible and acting on it will bring freedom to your life. We must hold to God's promises and use our faith to make them active in our lives (p 203).

2. As a Christian, you can have strongholds in your life that dominates and persecutes you. You may be ignorant of them, or you may be totally aware of them. God's goal is for you to live in freedom which requires you to have ears to hear Him when He uncovers any stronghold in your life (p 203).

3. Knowing, seeing, and agreeing. Once you know the truth and see your oppression, you must agree with the truth to establish freedom in your life (p 203).

4. True (p 203).

5. We can transition to a new spiritual level if the Body receives and walks in the truths released and revealed through dreams and visions (p 203).

6. Mature; childish (p 204).

7. Strong meat includes dreams and visions; it belongs to mature Christians and can be considered deep truths (p 203-204).

8. Agree; lies. We must cling to the truth of the Bible and walk in it daily (p 204).

9. To restore is "to be in covenant; to be safe; to be at peace; and to be complete." This is God's will for you! Varies (p 204).

10. The Holy Spirit (p 204).

11. Restoration brings us hope and peace through God's Spirit. Varies (p 204).

12. I kept being pulled into a life of anorexia. I would walk free of the pull for a period of time, but I would be pulled back into it. I needed the power over me to be broken; I needed deliverance (p 205).

13. *Chronos* time is the quantitative minutes of living out our daily lives. A *kairos* experience denotes a momentous occasion that impacts your future; it speaks of the right and opportune moment or an appointed time. There is no way to plan a *kairos* moment; however, as you go about life doing the right things—obeying the Word—God will meet you at an appointed time with your deliverance, your revelation, and your harvest (p 207).

14. Varies (p 204).

15. Varies. It's always appropriate to repent and pray. Resist the devil and he will flee (Ja 4:7). However, if there is a stronghold that has gained a fortified position in your life, you need divine assistance in this matter. It may help if you seek out a spiritual counsellor or pastor (p 205).

16. No, everything is not suddenly perfect. You still must walk out your deliverance. Deep wounds must be healed; habits have to be broken. Relationships must sometimes change. However, it's at this point of deliverance where the chains are broken and you have the grace, desire, and power to walk through the process to receive a manifestation of your total freedom (p 206-207).

17. Varies. Use your decree to cut down the enemy's strongholds in your life. Make your decree, and it will set you on your way to freedom (p 209-210).

18. Varies. "But if anyone obeys his word, love for God is truly made complete in them. This is how we know we are in him." (1 Jn 2:5, KJV). "And in Christ you have been brought to fullness" (Col 2:10).

19. Varies.

20. Varies.

21. You can get off the merry-go-round in your life by continuing to walk in your anointing. Use your anointing like the bumper car in my dream, and the devil will have to flee. Keep moving toward God, and Satan will have no place in your life. Varies (p 208-209).

Dream Journal

Date: _____   Time: _____   Recurring? _____   If so, when? _____

Dream Title: _____

Main Character: ⚪ Self   ⚪ Other: _____

Your Role: ⚪ Participant   ⚪ Observer

Colors: ⚪ B&W   ⚪ Vivid   ⚪ Muted   Color/s: _____

Location: _____

What's in the Background? _____

Emotions During the Dream:	Emotions Upon Awakening:
⚪ Fear ⚪ Dread	⚪ Fear ⚪ Dread
⚪ Joy ⚪ Excitement	⚪ Joy ⚪ Excitement
⚪ Other _____	⚪ Other _____

What's the Dream About?

List or Sketch Important Symbols

Pray for the Interpretation

REMEMBER:

"It is His perfect will for us to know His voice. Do not have a mindset about how God speaks. If we limit His ways of communication, we will not properly hear."
~ Sandie Freed

LESSON 12

MY GENERATIONAL JOURNEY TO FREEDOM

DREAM TEXT

I was finally free! And my complete freedom came through the voice of God in the night season. It has been many years now that I have not dealt with an illness on my birthday. I was delivered because of the Word of the Lord delivered through my dream (*Understanding Your Dreams*, 219).

DREAM FOCUS

I encourage you to refuse to stop short of total freedom. I received supernatural deliverance from the harmful lifestyle of anorexia and bulimia; however, I was still influenced by something I couldn't explain. Through a series of dreams, God showed me how the activities of my ancestors brought the consequences of their sin on me! Through revelation and prayer, the generational bondages that governed my life have been broken.

DREAM THINKING

1. In this chapter, I shared the roots of bondage that were causing the anorexia and bulimia in my life. What were these roots?

    1)_____

    2)_____

    3)_____

2. Can oppression keep you from ministering in your call to others?

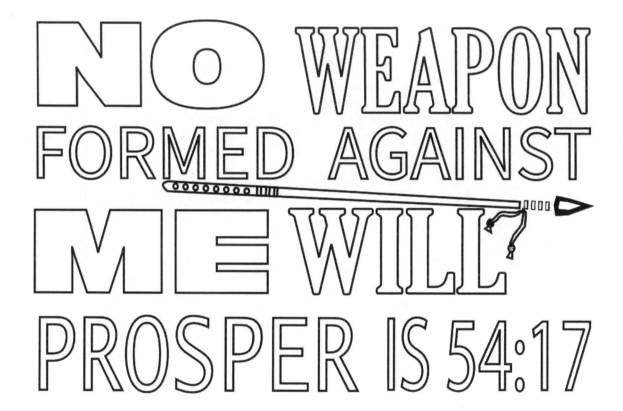

3.   What are the 2 "P" character traits that help when seeking the interpretation of a dream?

1)_____

2)_____

4.   I talk about a demonic assignment against my life in the terms: spirit of death or curse of death. What is this?

5.   Can you have a stronghold without having a generational curse?

6.   ☐ True   ☐ False   Satan could possibly have a legal right to intervene in a Christian's life. Explain your answer.

7.   List two sins through which the consequences can be passed down to future generations.

1)_____

2)_____

> GOD DOES NOT WANT TO PUNISH US. IN FACT, HIS DESIRE IS TO VISIT US THROUGH DREAMS SO THAT WE CAN BE DELIVERED, HEALED, AND RESTORED.

8.   I had root issues in my life (spirit of death, rejection, infirmity, abandonment) that came about from relatives speaking with the dead, holding séances, witchcraft, etc. How does a generational curse work? What Bible verse shows this truth?

9.   Why couldn't I just repent and be free of any generational curses?

10.   God showed me that three specific areas observed by my family that had given Satan a legal right to be in my life. What were these three areas?

       1)_____   _____

       2)_____

       3)_____

WALK in the FULLNESS of HIS CALLING

EPH 3:19

11.   Why do you think it took three dreams to lead me into total freedom?

12.   In this chapter, I list the 3 dreams that God used for me to push past the door of deliverance. What are the three dreams? Include a statement regarding how God used it to free me.

        1)_____

        2)_____

        3)_____

DREAM APPLICATION

13.   I included this testimony about my own generational curses so that you can see how consequences of your ancestor's actions possibly influence your life. God delivered me through dreams, and this can happen for you, too. How can you discern if long-standing issues in your life are generational? What are the steps to get rid of them once you are aware of them?

REMEMBER:

"Most dreams from God are given in metaphors and require interpretation."
~ Sandie Freed

14. Do you see how important it is to understand the correct interpretation of your dreams? As a review, in your own words, explain how to interpret your dreams accurately.

DREAM ACTIVATION

15. Take time to mediate on John 8:36 in various translations (see www.BibleHub.com). Like we did earlier, emphasize one word each time you repeat it. Insert your name in this verse. What revelation does God share about this truth? Think of areas in your life where you have experienced freedom and areas where you need freedom.

16. Do you have any knowledge of idolatry, mysticism, or witchcraft occurring in your family? Think about ungodly life-long behaviors that you see in your loved ones. Do you see any patterns? Write out a prayer to break those strongholds. Recite the prayer and believe God for freedom.

GOD WILL VISIT YOU IN DREAMS & REVEAL THE 'INIQUITY' OF THE GENERATIONS. THE WORD 'INIQUITY' MEANS A 'BENT'. IT IS REFERRING TO OUR HAVING A 'BENT' IN A CERTAIN DIRECTION OR HAVING A 'PROPENSITY' TO BE OR ACT A CERTAIN WAY.

17.   Ask God to reveal in your dreams any strongholds (gossiping, lying, addiction, etc) in you or your family. Write out your prayer and pray it; thank Him in faith believing for Him to do it. Include Bible verses in your prayer.

DREAM SHARING

18.   Have you been subject to having any nightmares or demonic inspired dreams? Do you know how to get rid of them? Explain. Discuss the steps you would use or have used to be free of this type of dream.

19.   Are you aware of any generational issues impacting your life? Have you ever experienced a dream that indicated an issue was generational? Share your experiences.

20.   From what you've learned, would you think that there are generational blessings in the same way that there are generational curses? Discuss this and include Bible verses.

DREAM ANSWERS - LESSON 12

1. Infirmity, rejection, abandonment (p 211).

2. It can, but not always. I was being oppressed, but I was still walking in my own anointing to minister to others. However, the more freedom you experience, the more God will be able to flow through you to others to meet their needs (p 211).

3. Patience, persistence (p 212).

4. It is a consolidated effort on behalf of evil forces to facilitate a premature death. A generational commission against your life that causes self-destructive behavior (suicide, anorexia, bulimia, drugs, alcohol, etc.) (p 212-213).

5. Yes, you can have a stronghold from sins you've practiced and the root is not in your family line. (p 212-214)

6. True. According to Exodus 20:5, iniquity of our ancestors can be passed down to the third and fourth generations (p 213). However, He who is freed by the Son is free indeed!

7. Some that are mentioned in this chapter are communicating with the dead (necromancy), summoning evil spirits (séances, black magic, Ouija Board™, familiar spirits), witchcraft, mysticism, idolatry (p 213-214).

8. A generational curse is a stronghold on a person where the enemy has a legal hold that originates from certain sins in which their ancestors participated (p 213). "I the Lord am a jealous God, visiting (avenging) the iniquity (sin, guilt) of the fathers upon the children [that is, calling the children to account for the sins of their fathers], to the third and fourth generations..." (Ex 20:5, AMPC).

9. I can repent for my personal sins; however, a generational sin or curse needs to be confessed and broken off. It has usually been around for a long time and gains a stronghold. Jesus gave you authority to tear down strongholds in His name. You, like me, may also need to be healed in your soul (p 214-215).

10. 1) Idolatry; 2) mysticism; 3) witchcraft (p 216).

11. You must have ears to hear as we discussed early on. God will only speak so much as we have the ears to hear or that we can understand. Each of the dreams brought me to a new revelation and finally after three dreams, I was able to apply the truths to reach total freedom in my life (p 218).

12. 1) Birthday dream—showed Satan placed a curse of death on me; 2) Dream of the desolate place—showed how Satan had a legal right in my life; 3) Dream of green corn ceremony—showed how my ancestors practiced idolatry (p 212-219).

13. If you have a bent or pulling to a certain ungodly lifestyle that has plagued your life, it's possible that you have a generational curse. This would be different than an occasional gossip or lie; however, a lifestyle consumed with gossip and lying could indicate a generational stronghold. You can receive your freedom by identifying the issue. Stay alert for God to speak to you in your dreams. Praying and breaking the power of the enemy over you in that area. Ask a faithful spiritual friend, counselor, or pastor to assist you in this area if you feel reinforcements are needed. Receive your freedom and choose to walk in it. You will most likely have to make certain changes in your life because this lifestyle may has become a habit. It may require a change in your relationships or your favorite places; you may need to add godly activities to your life to supplement the loss of your old sin. Jesus has made you free!! Now, you must truly allow that to permeate your entire spirit, soul, and body.

14. Varies. Record it. Ask God for understanding. Consult the Bible. Evaluate specifics. Symbols? Use dream language. Pray.

15. Varies.

16. Varies. Example of prayer for generational strongholds: "Thank you God for delivering me from the effects of idolatry, mysticism and witchcraft that was practiced in my family. I break any curse that is associated with these things in Jesus' Name. I refuse these sins and every evil work of the enemy in my life. Thank you for the name of Jesus to break the yoke that has bound me and the cleansing blood of Jesus that washes me clean. I choose to walk in the freedom that Jesus purchased for me because He who is freed by the Son is free indeed! Thank you, Lord." You may want to be anointed with oil to seal this matter.

17. Varies. Similar as above, but this prayer is for sins you have allowed to become a stronghold. Just start from the third sentence above. Greater is He in me (1 Jn 4:4); Christ set me free (Jn 8:36, Ga 5:1); resist the devil (Ja 4:7), God provides the way of escape (1 Cor 10:13); His yoke is easy (Mt 11:28-30).

18. Varies. Example: Pray. Bind the devil. Quote the Scripture. Sing worship songs. Anoint with oil. (See Lsn 6, #18 and Lsn 13, #10).

19. Varies.

20. Yes, generational blessings come from ancestors who served God and walked in His Word (Deut 28:1-14) (p 92).

Dream Journal

Date: _____ Time: _____ Recurring? _____ If so, when? _____

Dream Title: _____

Main Character: ⬤ Self   ⬤ Other: _____

Your Role: ⬤ Participant   ⬤ Observer

Colors: ⬤ B&W   ⬤ Vivid   ⬤ Muted   Color/s: _____

Location: _____

What's in the Background? _____

Emotions During the Dream:
⬤ Fear   ⬤ Dread
⬤ Joy   ⬤ Excitement
⬤ Other _____

Emotions Upon Awakening:
⬤ Fear   ⬤ Dread
⬤ Joy   ⬤ Excitement
⬤ Other _____

What's the Dream About?

List or Sketch Important Symbols

Pray for the Interpretation

> OUR ENEMY WANTS US TO BE TORMENTED WITH FEAR, BUT WE MUST NOT HIDE NOR RUN, BUT EMBRACE OUR SPIRITUAL AUTHORITY AND CONTINUE TO DEMONSTRATE KINGDOM AUTHORITY!

LESSON 13

GOD IS SPEAKING
TO OUR CHILDREN

DREAM TEXT

This book may be written for adults, but many of the truths and testimonies in it apply to the lives of children, too, and they can encourage and empower you to become a "life coach" to your own children as they encounter God in dreams and visions…So use what you have already learned, and have an open mind and heart as we finish this journey together. God wants to use your children for His glory just as much as He desires to use you! (*Understanding Your Dreams*, 222).

DREAM FOCUS

I want to encourage you to teach the children in your life about dreams. Let them know God loves them so much that He will speak to them in the night seasons. You will want to teach them about dreams that come from God and dreams from other sources. This is a great opportunity to help them establish an openness and reliance on the God they serve. Pay particular attention to this chapter so that you will have answers before issues arise. Dreams are an exciting part of the Christian life to position you and your child in line to fulfill divine destiny.

DREAM THINKING

1. The dreams of children may indicate occasions where they may cultivate their godly _____.

2. Why does God visit children in their dreams?

3. What are the three types of dream that a child (or adult) may have? Summarize each one.

    1)_____

    2)_____

    3)_____

4. A God-inspired dream is usually a message in a _____ requiring an _____ to understand.

5. When discussing the purpose of dreams from God, explain to your child that God:

    1) _____

    2) _____

    3) _____

    4) _____

    5) _____

6. ☐ True ☐ False   Sharing Bible stories about God speaking in visions and dreams can be scary to a child.

7. A great way to have a child recall a dream is to have them _____.

8. ☐ True ☐ False   It's fine to use a dream catcher to ward off bad dreams.

9. What are nightmares? Why do some people suffer from nightmares or demonically-inspired dreams?

"SATAN DESIRES TO ATTACK US, DERAIL US, SIDETRACK US, STEAL OUR VISION & BRING DEATH. BUT, LET'S REMEMBER THAT GOD PROMISES US LONG LIFE & THAT HE IS GIVING IT TO US IN ABUNDANCE!"

10.   How can you get rid of nightmares for yourself or a child?

11.   God may give a child a dream that exposes an area in his life that needs healing. If a child dreams about his dog biting him, what could this mean? If they had this dream, how could you minister to them?

12.   God reveals to always _____.

13.   How can God use a nightmare that we are having?

STEP INTO YOUR SPHERE OF AUTHORITY IN FAITH. KNOW THAT HE HAS ORDERED YOUR STEPS & THAT HE PROMISES TO EMPOWER YOU TO PUT EVERY ENEMY UNDERFOOT. THE BATTLE IS NOT YOURS ALONE—NO WAY!

14. How can you teach children to face their fears in a lucid dream? In a lucid dream, can you control the outcome of the dream?

15. ☐ Yes ☐ No Is it good to explore the interpretation of adult and child dreams together with your child? Explain your answer.

16. What is rescripting? How does it help you or a child with a nightmare?

17. ☐ True ☐ False The more interactive you are with a child's dream, the less trust and openness you build up.

18. Goals to remember when supervising your child's dreams are:

    1)_____

    2)_____

    3)_____

19. Dreams teach you and your child to take off all _____ because God is _____.

DREAM APPLICATION

20. What are two verses you can use if someone is having bad dreams or nightmares? Take time to recite these verses when you or your children have bad dreams or can't sleep.

RESIST the DEVIL &he WILL FLEE Ja 4:7

21.   Fear is a common emotional response to nightmares. Explain this statement: *God does not cause fear, but He can use it.*

DREAM ACTIVATION

22.   If you are involved in a child's life and they try to tell you about a dream, have you discouraged this or encouraged it?

23.   Make a list of Bible verses about defeating fear that you can teach your children.

"YOUR CHILDREN ARE BEING VISITED BY GOD BECAUSE HE LOVES THEM. WHEN THEY ARE QUIET & SETTLED DOWN AT NIGHT, HE WILL GIVE THEM DREAMS & SPEAK TO THEM CONCERNING THEIR FUTURE."

DREAM SHARING

24. Has the Lord used dreams to speak to your child or a child you know? What can you do to educate a child about their dreams? Have you ever had a dream you knew was for a child?

25. God gave my daughter a dream that resulted in saving my life. Have you ever experienced a time when your child or a child you know impacted your life in a huge way through dreams? If not, how could you cultivate this in your relationship?

26. Look over your text and study guide to review the table of contents. Think about any topics that you would like to review or discuss. Note areas that you need to work on. Make a conscious effort to receive the prayer I prayed for you at the end of this study guide (page 206). I am confident that as you walk in this knowledge and share it with others, God will be greatly pleased and glorified.

DREAM ANSWERS - LESSON 13

1. Identities (p 221).
2. He loves them, and children seem more open to spiritual things than some adults; they are full of faith to believe God would speak them (p 222-223).
3. 1) Demonic–extreme and scary; 2) soulish–involving your mind, will and emotions; involves selfish desires and ambitions; 3) godly–spiritual message (p 225-226).
4. Metaphor; interpretation (p 226).
5. 1) Communicates; 2) leads and guides us; 3) reveals distractions that subvert His will; 4) speaks in a still, small voice; 5) speaks in visions (p 226).
6. False. The story and your explanation will help to elevate the child's faith and desire for God to speak with them in dreams and visions (p 226-227).
7. Draw it (p 227).
8. False. Dream catchers are based in folklore and fantasy and can possibly make the dreams worse (p 228).
9. Nightmares bring fear, panic, coercion, and anxiety which usually involves a danger. It may indicate a generational curse that needs to be broken (p 119-120, 228).
10. Anoint your threshold and bedpost with oil to bring God's presence on the scene. You can sing songs about the blood of Jesus and His victory over Satan. Pray for peace and protection while taking your authority to force out the enemy from your/their sleep. For a child, you need to teach them that God does not cause fear; if you're afraid, it's not God. Then, you can teach them to face their fear and command the devil to flee (p 120, 229).
11. It could mean that he is ashamed and deserving of a reprimand; he may feel he is unworthy. You should teach them about repentance and God's unfailing love and forgiveness. We all mess up, and we all need God's help to live a life pleasing to Him (p 230).
12. Heal (p 231).
13. God can use a nightmare to show us an area of weakness (i.e. fear) so that we can take authority over it. The more authority we walk in, the more authority God will bestow on us . Use this opportunity to teach your children about their authority as a Christian (p 231). See Lsn 6, #17.
14. You can teach them to face their fears and gain control of a situation by revisiting a lucid dream and changing outcome. Yes, you can often control the dream's end once you fall back to sleep and continue that dream (p 120-121, 233). See Lsn 6, #13.
15. Yes, it is a great opportunity for you and your child to mutually share about dreams. It creates an atmosphere of trust and creativity to explore God's message through His Word. Both parent and child will grow during these times (p 235).
16. Rescripting is a role-playing exercise while awake to come up with a new ending to a dream. It's like a do-over. This will allow you or your child to determine the appropriate and God-inspired ending. This exercise keeps one's attention off of fear and on who you are in Christ and His victory (p 237).
17. False. The more you talk to a child about their dreams, the more they will want to communicate with you about them. Welcome your child's dreams, and the journey will endow him with the ability to overcome and walk in victory. It will also open your child up to God's supernatural dealings in a safe environment (p 240).
18. 1) Establish a relationship with the Lord; 2) emotional well-being; 3) cultivate creativity (p 241).
19. Limits; unlimited or limitless (p 241).
20. Varies. Prov 3:24; Phil 4:7; Ecc 5:12; Ps 4:8 (KJV); Ps 127:2. Use these verses when having trouble sleeping.
21. God can use things that cause us fear to teach us about spiritual authority and show us areas where we need victory. Remember what the devil means for evil, God can turn it to good (Ge 50:20) (p 229).
22. Varies. From now on, you will hopefully encourage it (p 235-237).
23. Varies. 1 Jn 4:18; Ps 3:6; Ps 23:4; Ps 118:6; 1 Pe 3:14. These verses also work well when having trouble sleeping.
24. Varies.
25. Varies.
26. Varies.

Dream Journal

Date: ⬭⬭⬭   Time: ⬭⬭⬭   Recurring? ⬭⬭⬭   If so, when? ⬭⬭⬭

Dream Title: ⬭⬭⬭⬭⬭⬭⬭⬭⬭

Main Character: ⬤ Self   ⬤ Other: _____

Your Role: ⬤ Participant   ⬤ Observer

Colors: ⬤ B&W   ⬤ Vivid   ⬤ Muted   Color/s: _____

Location: _____

What's in the Background? _____

Emotions During the Dream:

⬤ Fear   ⬤ Dread

⬤ Joy   ⬤ Excitement

⬤ Other _____

Emotions Upon Awakening:

⬤ Fear   ⬤ Dread

⬤ Joy   ⬤ Excitement

⬤ Other _____

What's the Dream About?

List or Sketch Important Symbols

Pray for the Interpretation

A SPECIAL PRAYER FOR YOU

Allow me to pray for you: Father God, I want to thank You for the many times that You have addressed our generational strongholds through our dreams and visions. Thank You for revealing our shame, our addictions, our idolatry, and our sins through revelation in our dreams. Lord, You desire that each of us experience divine healing and deliverance. You even reveal our future through dreams. Thank You for heavenly encounters through our dreams and visions. Lord, each of us expects a divine visitation through our dreams and visions! In Jesus' name, amen!

ABOUT THE AUTHOR

Dr. Sandie Freed is an internationally recognized speaker and author of over twelve books. Her passion is to empower others to experience freedom in Christ and to impart life transformation to God's people. Sandie always speaks from her heart; her revelation and transparency will captivate your heart to shift into divine purpose. She releases a powerful anointing of healing and hope to those who have been held captive. With a strong anointing of discerning of spirits, Sandie has been known to discern territorial strongholds and release churches and regions from spiritual assignments that withhold finances, deliverance, and breakthroughs. She is also known for her "cutting-edge" prophetic ministry, and she also moves very strongly in words of knowledge and miracles.

As a modern day Joseph in dream interpretation, she has become particularly anointed in releasing and activating dreams and visions as well as being strongly gifted with the interpretation. She has hosted and has ministered in numerous Dreams and Visions seminars, whereby she teaches and trains others to interpret dreams. Sandie has been featured numerous times on various radio broadcasts as well as Daystar's "Celebration" program and "Life Today" with James Robinson. In addition to interviews regarding Dreams and Visions, other topics about which Sandie speaks include Overcoming Eating Disorders and Generational Strongholds. Her powerful testimony has ministered to thousands world-wide.

Sandie has traveled nationally and internationally teaching on spiritual discernment. Her ability to accurately prophesy and discern spiritual strongholds over regions has released numerous breakthroughs for individuals and ministries.

Dr. Sandie and Apostle/Pastor Mickey are ordained with Christian International Ministries, serving on their Board of Governors. Sandie presently co-pastors with her husband, Mickey, at Lifegate Church International in Hurst, Texas. They have been married since 1973 and have one daughter, Kimberly; a son-in-law, Daniel Wheeler; and two wonderful grandchildren, Elijah and Perrin Wheeler.

Understanding Your Dreams—How to Unlock the Meaning of God's Messages

Spoken in the language of heaven—the language of our spirits—dreams and visions can be revelations from God that connect straight to your heart. He can use them to reveal your future, heal your soul, draw you closer to Him, impart direction and guidance, expose and defeat strongholds, and empower you to step into your true purpose and destiny.

Laying out a biblical framework for interpreting these nighttime messages, pastor and author Sandie Freed helps you translate this beautiful language and discover how to:
- prepare to hear from God
- discern the source of your dreams
- identify and interpret the context, type, symbols, numbers, colors and objects
- protect, battle and bless your dreams
- apply God's messages to your life
- empower your children to understand their dreams
- and more!

ISBN: 978-0800794200

Chosen Books

Visit my website at www.SandieFreed.com for additional dream journal pages.

Sandie Freed Books

 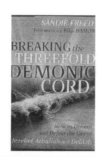 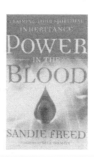 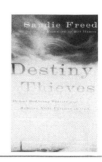

Faith After Failure: Reconnecting with Your Destiny

Failure. It knocks at the doors of our lives and hopes to find permanent residence. The haunting words regarding past failures and doubts resound over and over in our minds until we come to the realization that in God there is no failure! Every obstacle in life is an opportunity for our faith to be renewed and witness the miracle of God's transforming power. God doesn't expect perfection; in fact, He seeks to prove His love and faithfulness by perfecting us as we walk through the challenges of life. This book is all about the times we find ourselves in the pit of despair and are then equipped by God's grace to move forward once again and experience complete fulfillment in Christ. There is no mission impossible for God.

ISBN: 978-1602730557   Parsons Publishing House

Breaking the Threefold Demonic Cord

God has a divine plan to release his people from the curse of desolation and barrenness. Satan also has a strategy, however, which is to lock us to our past. He uses a three-fold cord of strongholds that seek to destroy us from victorious Christian living. But by exposing the plans of the enemy, God's people can be released from barrenness and launched into expansion, growth, and multiplication. Sandie Freed takes readers through a close study of each of these demonic forces in order to prepare them to break the threefold demonic cord. Conducting a biblical exploration of the everyday tactics of each spirit, Freed lays bare their strategies and helps readers defeat them through prayer.

ISBN: 978-0800794361   Chosen Books

Power in the Blood: Claiming Your Spiritual Inheritance

Spiritual Warfare Expert Helps Believers Claim Their Spiritual Inheritance. What Christians often forget is that they are royalty—children of the one true King. They are royalty not through works but through Jesus' blood, the blood that bought them, that saved them. And in his blood is their inheritance: eternal life, authority, destiny, wisdom, and more! With a discerning perspective gained from years in spiritual warfare and prophetic ministry, Sandie Freed offers life-transforming advice on how believers can rediscover their spiritual ancestry, awaken to their royal identities, and claim the inheritance God is holding for them.

ISBN: 978-0800795511   Chosen Books

Destiny Thieves

God has a plan for every one of his children, but there are powers working against this plan that attempt to subvert the destiny of believers. Just as Adam and Eve were seduced into sin by the serpent, Christians today still experience these destructive powers that threaten to steal their divine destiny. In this book, Sandie Freed shares the story of her own struggle, as well as many biblical accounts of the struggles of God's people, with the demonically-inspired obstacles that stand in the way of breakthrough. This liberating book shows readers the tactics Satan uses against believers, identifies particular seducing spirits, and charges believers with a new level of faith to go forward and claim the victorious life God has planned for them.

ISBN: 978-0800794200   Chosen Books

Sandie Freed Books

 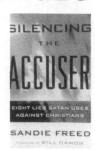

NEW
COVER
COMING
SOON

The Jezebel Yoke: Breaking Free from Bondage and Deception

Since the Garden of Eden, God's children have let the Deceiver seduce them away from their rightful blessings and, as a result, their true identities. Most are not even aware they are being deceived. With her trademark boldness and warmth, respected spiritual warfare expert Sandie Freed exposes spirits of deception--including Jezebel, Belial, Ahab, and more--and the tactics these demonic entities use to steal Christians' spiritual birthright. She also provides clarity and insight into the many ways believers are deceived and offers keys to inviting God's blessing. By showing readers how to shift back into their divine destinies, Sandie once again delivers a book that will set believers down the road to freedom.

ISBN: 978-0800795252

Chosen Books

Silencing the Accuser: Eight Lies Satan Uses Against Christians

Many Christians are unaware of the lies Satan, the accuser, whispers in their ears. Not only does he accuse believers, but he deceives them concerning their relationships with God and their identities. Using the Old Testament story of Job, author Sandie Freed exposes our ancient enemy and the multiple ways he manipulates believers. With her trademark transparency and warmth, Freed encourages those struggling with a sense of hopelessness, a negative self-image, or a season of attacks--to name just three. She shows readers how to root out and overcome the negative thoughts the accuser plants, arming them with battle-tested prayer strategies to silence him and his deadly whisperings forever.

ISBN: 978-0800795108

Chosen Books

How to Operate in God's Kingdom Wealth: Defeating the Strategies of Mammon

This book provides a fresh perspective on the biblical messages of "Where your treasure is, there your heart will be also" and "The love of money is a root of all kinds of evil." Sandie Freed reveals how to work within God's financial framework for Kingdom wealth. With insight and wisdom, Freed exposes the seductive power of mammon. She arms readers to fight these strongholds with the powerful Word of God and real life, personal examples of victory as she shows them how to break their bondages to wealth, riches, status, and anxiety over finances. Not a book on how to create a budget, make money, or invest wisely, this release empowers readers to seek God's wisdom and favor concerning wealth. Only then can believers find financial and spiritual freedom. Formerly published under the title of: *Crushing the Spirits of Greed and Poverty*.

ISBN: 978-1602731004

Parsons Publishing House

Heaven's Voice

Do you want to hear from Heaven? Of course you do! That's why this book is another must-read by Sandie Freed. Known for her humor in sharing her life experiences and her prophetic insight, Sandie has once again penned her revelation to mobilize the Church into victory. Heaven has a distinctive language, and the Lord desires that we hear the sound of Heaven and shift into our future. This book is packed full of revelation to empower you to hear and understand how God is speaking today through sounds. Topics include: how to have spiritual ears, how to recognize the sound of war, and how to shift as a Third Day church.

ISBN: 978-0939868520

Kingdom Word Publishers